Colorado Treasure Tales

Other Caxton titles by
W. C. Jameson:

New Mexico Treasure Tales
ISBN 0-87004-429-x

COLORADO TREASURE TALES

W. C. Jameson

CAXTON PRESS
Caldwell, Idaho
2005

Second Printing, May 2005

Library of Congress Cataloging-in-Publication Data

Jameson, W. C., 1942-
   Colorado treasure tales / W.C. Jameson.
     p. cm.
   Includes bibliographical references (p.).
   ISBN 0-87004-402-8 (alk. paper)
   1. Colorado--History, Local--Anecdotes. 2.
Treasure-trove--Colorado--History--Anecdotes.   I. Title.
  F776.6 .J36 2001
  978.8--dc21
                        2001047178

Lithographed and bound in the United States of America by
CAXTON PRESS
Caldwell, Idaho
172274

This book is dedicated to
Jameson Richard Lajoie.

May your life be filled with
adventures such as these.

CONTENTS

MAPS

INTRODUCTION

Since the beginning of recorded history, tales and legends of lost mines and buried and sunken treasures have held an incredible fascination and appeal for most people. The reading about or the search for a lost mine or buried treasure excites men and women, young and old, and the attraction to such things has not dimmed over time. Indeed, if anything, it has increased. To this day we remain spellbound by the legend of King Solomon's mines, by stories of sunken treasures off the coast of Florida, by Arizona's Lost Dutchman Mine, by lost Spanish treasures in Texas and Mexico, and by the dozens of such tales that have as their setting the state of Colorado.

In North America, such tales and legends likely had their beginnings with the earliest exploration by the French and Spanish. Though the legendary golden city of El Dorado was never found, if, in fact, it ever existed, tons of gold and silver were nevertheless extracted from the rocks and panned from the streams of this continent, with Colorado being the center for much of this activity. In the wake of the Spaniards and Frenchmen came others who found more of the precious ore, sometimes on purpose and sometimes by complete accident.

In some cases the old mines are still there, many of them located in remote areas high up on mountainsides and at the end of seldom traveled and overgrown trails. They are difficult to locate and even more difficult to reach. Some still have gold and silver in them, rich ore awaiting the lucky finder. Some of them are empty, save for a discarded tool here and there. The metal has been mined out and the miners gone. Though many, if not most, of these locations have long been abandoned, what always remains are the stories: The tales, the lore, and the legends handed down over the generations as part of the oral tradition, other times tucked away in journals and diaries, and sometimes found in published books. In many ways the tales themselves are much like the ore in that, culturally speaking, they represent a portion of the wealth of the people. In many ways they are priceless.

The great state of Colorado is considered by many to be the Holy Grail of lost mines and buried treasures for the United States.

It has been argued that more lost gold and silver mines, buried caches of outlaw loot, and long-hidden hoards of Spanish and French treasures exist in Colorado than any of the remaining United States. The incredible number of tantalizing folktales, legends, and stories of lost and buried wealth that have come out of the state would certainly support this contention. Year in and year out, these tales and legends attract to Colorado professional treasure hunters, experienced miners, and weekend prospectors, all searching for the wealth that has lured them. Wealth that, in fact, excites and lures all of us.

In a few cases, some of these lost mines and buried treasures are found, and the searcher returns home a richer person. In other cases people come searching for the stories, the tales, and the legends. The search for such may not involve traveling to remote locations along abandoned trails, but it can involve the adventure of exploring through libraries, old journals and diaries, and interviewing those who have actually participated in the search or who may be descended from one or more of the principals in one of the stories.

That gold and silver were mined in Colorado in great abundance cannot be argued. Starting with the earliest French and Spanish explorers and miners of centuries ago, the precious metals were extracted from the rocks, from the mountains, from the hillsides, and panned from the hundreds of streams that flow out of the Rocky Mountains.

It has been documented time and again that French and Spanish explorers in this area found gold and silver and opened mines and mining camps. Uncountable tons of ore were dug from the rock, smelted into ingots, and transported back to Mexico and, as was often the case, across the Atlantic Ocean to Spain.

It has also been documented that many of the Spanish mines were closed and abandoned as a result of increasing Indian hostilities in the region beginning around the mid-1670s and continuing for well over a century.

The historical record is replete with accounts of gold and silver discoveries in Colorado by early settlers, prospectors, miners, and engineers. Hundreds, if not thousands, of mines were operated, some producing untold millions of dollars worth of ore.

Abundant evidence also exists that substantiates the claims that tons of gold and silver, transported via mule, burro, horseback, coach, and train were carried from the mines and smelters to a variety of destinations ranging from Mexico City to Europe to the United States Mint in Philadelphia. A great deal of this wealth never arrived at its destinations, and history reveals that much of it was stolen by highwaymen, a large percentage of which was cached. And sometimes lost.

To this day, lost and buried gold, silver, coins, jewelry, and other treasures are occasionally discovered. Hundreds of millions of dollars worth of gold, silver and precious artifacts have been retrieved from the Colorado Rockies to the continental shelves of the western and eastern United States. Many of those who have recovered lost and buried treasures have been wealthy entrepreneurs, or have been businessmen who were successful in soliciting the backing of wealthy entrepreneurs.

On the other hand, a significant amount of lost and buried treasure has also been discovered by average citizens. Treasure hunters, both professional and amateur, unearth amazing fortunes year in and year out.

A great deal of treasure is also found completely by accident. The annals are filled with accounts of hikers, backpackers, hunters, or just someone strolling down a remote trail and coming across some lost or buried treasure.

Whether or not one finds the lost or hidden gold and silver is more often than not a matter of chance. Though the searchers for this wealth often come away empty-handed in terms of material wealth, they are richer by far for having had the experience of the quest, and particularly for having had the experience with the story itself.

Tales and legends of lost mines and buried treasures are handed down from generation to generation and over the centuries by the members of the various cultures that exist around the world. All cultures throughout history possessed such tales and legends, and they are as much a fabric of a society as any other cultural element including religion, food, drink, dancing, music, architecture, or language. They are cultural, they are enduring, and they permeate civilizations from Rangoon to Baltimore.

For many of us, the stories are where it all starts. Many a youngster in this country became excited about reading as a result of being handed a book about lost mines and buried treasures. Many an old-timer plans a vacation around a search for some lost mine or buried treasure. Some of us read the tales and the legends simply for the pure pleasure of it. In the books themselves can be found immense treasures.

And every so often, some of us, as a result of our reading and study and research and patience, actually find some of the treasure.

This book represents a collection of some of the more intriguing, mysterious, and compelling tales of lost mines and buried treasures in the state of Colorado. They represent some of the best stories collected, researched, and searched over four decades. Chasing down the facts related to these stories and searching for the actual mines and treasures themselves lured me to Colorado and has lured me back again and again. There were some expeditions that met with success, and others that met with failure, but with each we came away richer with the experience of this wonderful place. In uncountable ways, Colorado itself is an awesome treasure.

Colorado is a state that possesses a rich and varied landscape, and is naturally divided into unique regions, each with their own compelling geology, culture, and charm. This book, therefore, is divided much like the state of Colorado, into natural geographic regions, with each section treating a particular natural division. They are the Western Slope, the Northern Rockies, the Southern Rockies, and the Eastern Plains.

The first section deals with what Colorado natives refer to as the Western Slope, that portion of the state located west of the foothills of the dominant chains of Rocky Mountains that run more or less north-south down the center of the state.

Next comes the Northern Rockies. So vast are the Colorado Rocky Mountains, and so rich in the lore and legend of lost mines and buried treasures, that it becomes necessary to divide them in half. The Northern Rockies comprise the Rocky Mountains in the northern half of the state and include ranges such as the Medicine Bow Mountains, the Front Range, and portions of the Gore Range, the Elk Mountains, and the Sawatch Range.

The Southern Rockies include the San Juan Mountains and portions of the Sangre de Cristo Mountains, the Sawatch Mountains, and the Elk Mountains.

The Eastern Plains begin approximately where Interstate 25 bisects the state and continue to the Nebraska and Kansas borders. Though geographers consider this to be part of the Great Plains, the Eastern Plains of Colorado are cut up into a number of canyons and impressive river valleys by many eastward-flowing streams.

Via this book the reader is invited to sit back and embark on a series of expeditions into Colorado, to join me in the search for lost mines and buried treasures.

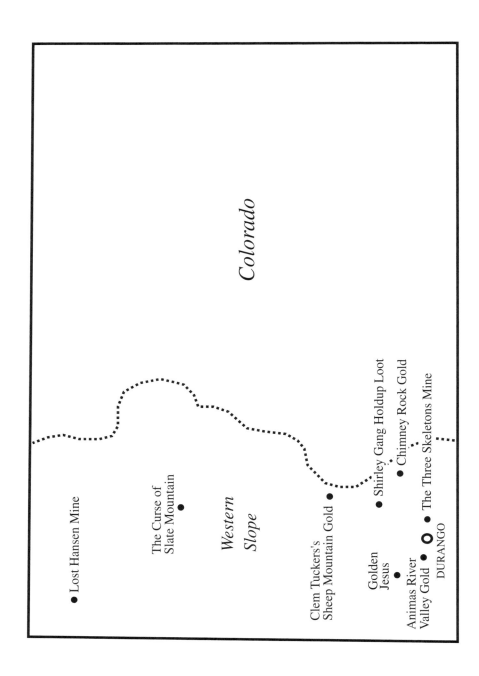

THE WESTERN SLOPE

The natural division of Colorado that geographers refer to as the Western Slope begins just west of the continental divide and continues Pacificward to the border shared with Utah. Most of the Western Slope is made up of a geological province known as the Colorado Plateau, a region that has been uplifted as much as three miles since the Cretaceous Period of approximately one hundred million years ago. The remainder of the Western Slope is comprised of the southern part of another geologic province called the Wyoming Basin as well as a small portion of the Middle Rocky Mountains, all of which are similar to the Colorado Plateau in appearance.

The Colorado Plateau is distinguished by a variety of geomorphic features, the most dominant of which are the extensive areas of nearly horizontal layers of sedimentary rock. This rather soft rock has been effectively and extensively incised by fast-flowing streams, forming steep canyons and hogbacks. In the southern part of the Colorado Plateau in Arizona can be found extreme examples of these incisions, namely the Grand Canyon and its associated structures.

Throughout this environment can also be found abundant evidence of previous volcanic activity: Numerous dormant and dead volcanoes, volcanic necks, and high lava-capped plateaus and mesas.

Aridity dominates this land, giving rise to sparse vegetation and extensive areas of bare, exposed rock. This shortage of water has also served to inhibit any significant human settlement in the area for generations. Even today, the current population density in Colorado's Western Slope is estimated to be only six people per square mile.

Mineral extraction has been undertaken in parts of the Western Slope since early settlers first arrived in the area. Though the region does not compare to the Northern and Southern Colorado Rockies when it comes to extensive deposits of precious metals, it nevertheless has yielded impressive quantities of uranium, coal, oil, gas, and potash. Production of other minerals such as gold and silver has been described by most geologists as "minor."

It is well known that early Spanish explorers passed through portions of the Colorado Plateau in search of settlement possibilities as well as for deposits of gold and silver. Evidence of their abbreviated mining activities can still be found to this day, but abundant evidence shows that they failed to harvest enough ore from the Western Slope to encourage permanent settlement. Eventually, they moved eastward into the heart of the Rocky Mountain chain that runs through the center of the state.

Though occasional tales describing impressive deposits of precious metals have come out of this region, and even though some small amounts of gold and silver have, indeed, been found here, the quantities have not inspired any kind of extensive and prolonged mining activity.

Because of the sparse population that exists in the Western Slope, outlaws have historically found it to be a relatively safe haven, far from the pursuit of lawmen.

Travelers through this sparsely settled region often fell prey to the highwaymen, and accounts of robberies and lost and buried outlaw booty are widespread and numerous.

Extensive portions of the Western Slope have been described as consisting of rugged, somewhat forbidding environments. In spite of this characterization, or perhaps because of it, this unique geographic region has been an important source of many compelling tales of lost mines and buried treasures.

THE THREE SKELETONS MINE

One of the greatest mysteries in the annals of Colorado lost mine and buried treasure lore has to do with what has come to be called the Three Skeletons Mine. Somewhere near Bear Creek, located some thirty miles from Durango, lies a mine shaft that has produced impressive quantities of very rich gold. In addition to the gold, the shaft also contains the skeletons of three men. To this day, the location of this shaft remains a mystery, as do the identities of the three skeletons.

* * *

In 1905, a lone man whose name has been lost to history, led a supplies-laden burro through the seldom-visited valley of Bear Creek in southwestern Colorado near Durango. The prospector was finding traces of gold here and there in the foothills. Indeed, he had occasionally panned small amounts from the streams in this region, just enough to get by. He remained ever hopeful of making the big strike that always seemed to elude him. On the morning of his third day in this particular area, his wanderings took him to a very old and abandoned mine shaft. Curious, he entered the tunnel and examined it.

Inside the dark shaft, the prospector found abundant evidence of a very active mine. Curiously, tools were scattered across the floor of the tunnel as if the miners who worked here had been compelled to leave in a hurry. The shoring he found in the shaft consisted of once-stout logs obviously cut from the nearby forest. The timbers were quite rotten, further testimony to the notion that this mine had been worked a long, long time ago. Approximately fifty feet inside the mine shaft, he found two piles of gold nuggets, each nearly one foot high. It appeared as though the gold had been collected there then placed into some kind of container. On inspecting the ore, he found it to be very rich. He placed a quantity of the gold in each of the the ore sacks he carried in his belt. After the sacks were filled, there remained on the floor enough gold to fill several more.

The prospector assumed the gold he found on the floor came from a vein at the back of the mine, so he proceeded to search for it. Fashioning a torch from some dried grasses and sticks of pine, he proceeded along the shaft until he came to a sight that caused him to freeze in terror. There, on the floor of the tunnel just ahead, were the skeletons of three men, long dead, their garments rotted and in tatters and hanging from their bones.

Unnerved somewhat by his encounter with the human remains, the prospector backed away. On exiting the mine shaft, he paused long enough to regain his composure, then decided he would take what gold he had to Durango, convert it to cash, and return to the mine some time later to continue his search for the rich vein he was certain existed at the end of the tunnel.

On arriving in Durango, the prospector had the gold assayed and then sold it to a local smelter for cash. He was asked where he found the gold several times by individuals who saw it, but, aside from describing the mine itself, along with the skeletons and the ore on the floor, the prospector only provided cryptic answers relative to the location. He answered the queries by saying only that it was somewhere near Bear Creek. After purchasing some mining supplies and several week's worth of provisions, the prospector departed Durango and headed back to the Bear Creek area.

The prospector was never seen again and his fate is unknown. Several years later, a skeleton was found next to an old campsite near the trail to Bear Creek. Some of the gear found near the skeleton was similar to the tools and other items the prospector purchased in Durango, thus many have concluded the poor man met his end before he ever made it back to Bear Creek to mine the gold.

In May 1918, a young man named Pedro Martinez arrived in Durango with a quantity of gold he wanted to sell. When pressed for details, Martinez said that while he was out deer hunting near Bear Creek he discovered an old, abandoned mine shaft. To the amazement of those who questioned him, he stated that he merely picked the gold up from a pile he found in the middle of the floor of the shaft. His description of the mine was very similar to the one provided by the prospector who sold the gold in Durango thirteen years earlier, including the discovery of the three skeletons.

A group of entrepreneurs approached Martinez with an impressive offer of money if he would lead them to the mine, but the young man refused. His refusal, interestingly, was based on his belief that the presence of skeletons suggested that the mine was haunted and protected by spirits, and that for him to reveal its location to anyone would bring bad luck.

Apparently his fear of spirits did not keep Martinez from returning to the mine, for each time he came to Durango he carried with him a quantity of the same kind of gold which he always converted to cash.

Within a few days of following his latest return to Durango, Martinez came down with a severe case of influenza, one serious enough to confine him to bed for two weeks. At the end of that time, Martinez died, and with him went any information on the location of what Durango residents were now calling the Three Skeletons Mine.

In the summer of 1938, a local sheepherder brought a coffee can full of gold into Durango and asked questions about how he could go about turning it into cash. A few who had dealings with Pedro Martinez twenty years earlier recognized the gold as similar to that brought to town by the Mexican. When asked where he found the gold, the sheepherder told about finding an abandoned shaft near Bear Creek, one that contained rotting timbers, abandoned tools, and three skeletons!

This time, when approached by investors, the sheepherder agreed to lead a party of men to the mine in exchange for a large payment in cash. Apparently, on nearing the mine the sheepherder had a change of heart, for he kept insisting he was lost and disoriented and unable to relocate the old shaft. The investors, angered by this turn of events, threatened to have the sheepherder killed on the spot if they were not taken to the mine. Late that night after the members of the party had gone to sleep, the sheepherder gathered up his belongings and fled into the darkness, never to be seen in the vicinity again. Though never verified, it was reported he had traveled to California and moved in with his sister's family.

To this day, no one has uncovered any information per-taining to the original operators of the mine or how much gold was taken from it. The identity of the three skeletons is likewise a mystery.

Most versions of the Three Skeletons Mine end with the disappearance of the unnamed sheepherder. There is, however, a little known addendum to this tale.

The year was 1945, and a young man arrived in Durango with a quartz-bearing rock about the size of a football. Throughout the quartz ran spidery seams of what appeared to be pure gold.

The young man entered a cafe, placed the rock on the lunch counter, and asked the proprietor if he could tell him whether or not the seams were gold. The proprietor looked the rock over closely and said it sure looked like gold to him and asked the newcomer where he found it.

Amazingly, the young man told a strange tale of extracting it from a thick vein he found in an old mine he located out near Bear Creek. If this was gold, he boasted, then there was enough of it left in the mine to make millionaires of more than a dozen men. In addition to the gold, he said the mine also contained a quantity of very old tools, rotting timbers, and three skeletons!

At this point, a diner seated nearby, a man of approximately fifty years of age, finished his lunch and came over to inspect the rock. He identified himself as a geologist and said the rock contained only fool's gold, not real gold. Disheartened, the young man left the rock at the cafe and was never seen again. The proprietor placed the rock on a nearby shelf and displayed it as a curiosity.

Several months later, a traveler seated at the counter eating lunch noticed the rock and asked to see it up close. The proprietor placed it on the counter and the newcomer examined it closely for several minutes. Presently, he asked the man behind the counter where it came from.

The proprietor related the story told by the young man and the identification of the rock provided by the gent who claimed he was a geologist.

The diner who was inspecting the rock stated that no real geologist would ever identify this as fool's gold. It was, he said, real gold of a most pure variety and would assay out at a very high value.

To date, there is no evidence that anyone has rediscovered The Three Skeletons Mine. Should someone come upon it, there awaits an incredible fortune in rich gold at the end of the tunnel.

Clem Tucker's Sheep Mountain Gold

Somewhere on or very near Sheep Mountain in the western part of the state of Colorado is a long-lost gold mine, one that yielded an impressive quantity of gold sometime prior to the Civil War, and one that has long since been lost. Based on what is known about this mine, whomever happens to eventually locate it would likely become one of the wealthiest persons in North America.

*   *   *

The beginnings of this story are rooted in the person of Dora Tucker Cyre, a young woman who moved to Central City, Colorado, from her childhood home in Independence, Missouri, sometime during the 1850s. Tucker was twenty-two years old and newly married to a printer named George Cyre who had taken a job with the Central City newspaper.

Dora resisted the move, not wanting to leave the relative security of family and friends in Independence, the only home she had known. On arriving in Central City, located about twenty miles west of Denver, she was at first quite intimidated by the tall mountains and rugged landscapes. Furthermore, she remained nervous about the proximity to what she perceived to be threatening wildlife such as grizzly bears, wolves, and mountain lions. Stories of hostile Indians living within just a few miles of Central City did little to relieve the tension she felt about her new residence.

After one year in Central City, George Cyre took a new job at a newspaper in Golden, some ten miles closer to Denver. George and Dora were busy getting settled into their new environs when tragedy struck. One evening after work, George became involved in an argument at a Golden tavern and was stabbed to death. Dora, married for slightly more than a year, now found herself a widow.

George did not leave Dora much in the way of money or possessions, and it took her only a few days to realize she was nearly destitute. Her first inclination was to return to her family in Missouri, but she didn't even have enough money to purchase a train ticket. Her pride kept her from wiring her family to request funds, a decision she would soon regret. Desperate and fearful, Dora remarried within a month a miner named Clem Tucker. Tucker, a prospector and loner who was generally avoided by most of Golden's residents, made a living of sorts by panning some gold from the area streams. He proposed marriage to Dora one afternoon when he was drunk and was quite surprised when she accepted.

Tucker has been described as somewhat coarse in manner and language, uneducated, and unkempt. Some have suggested that Tucker sensed Dora's vulnerability and took advantage of it. Whatever the case, it was not long before Dora realized she had made a terrible mistake.

Two days after their wedding, Tucker packed their few belongings onto his two mules and together the newlyweds walked the 200 miles to Sheep Mountain where he had been prospecting for gold. Dora was miserable during the entire journey, enduring blisters, fatigue, sunburn, and cold weather. When she had difficulty keeping up with the experienced Tucker, he cursed and whipped her. At night when they made camp, the exhausted Dora was forced to make the campfire and prepare the evening meal while Tucker rested and smoked his pipe.

When they finally arrived at Sheep Mountain, Tucker made Dora maintain the crude camp at which they resided, their home being merely a ripped and ragged canvas tent pitched on a rocky and uneven surface. Eventually, Tucker forced her to wield a pick and shovel to aid him in his search for gold. When Dora complained of the heavy work, or when she simply collapsed from sheer exhaustion, Tucker beat her repeatedly, oftentimes leaving her unconscious. Finally summoning the courage to address him, Dora told Tucker she was not satisfied with the marriage and wished to return to Golden. Tucker informed her that she was obligated to him and that if she ever tried to leave he would kill her.

On awakening one morning several weeks after coming to Sheep Mountain, Tucker noticed that one of his mules had wandered away. After breakfast, he set out to look for it. He finally located the mule about two hours later in a canyon two miles away, one he had never explored or prospected. As he was leading the animal out of the canyon, he was suddenly distracted by a reflection of sunlight from a nearby rock outcrop. When Tucker went to investigate the source of the reflection, he was startled to discover a thick vein of quartz laced throughout with the purest gold he had ever encountered.

For the next few weeks, Tucker, leaving Dora to tend camp, dug gold from the outcrop, eventually excavating a narrow shaft which followed the seam approximately twenty feet into the rock. Each night he would return to camp and spread his newly acquired gold out across a blanket and stare at it for hours before falling asleep. One night he informed Dora that he had excavated enough gold to make him a very rich man. He told her that within the month he was going to travel to Denver to purchase some mining equipment and would be gone for several weeks. She was, he told her, to remain in camp during that time and tend to things.

Dora could not imagine living in this remote location by herself for weeks at a time—the more she thought about it the more frightened she became. Her fear of being alone in the wilderness, however, was not as great as her fear of Tucker, and she determined she could not spend another month with this vicious man. She decided she must do something to get away from her vicious brute of a husband.

That night she watched as Tucker spread out his gold and admired it. Presently, he placed it in a flour sack with some of the ore he mined earlier in the week. Carrying the sack just a few feet from the camp, Tucker buried it in a shallow hole, one already filled with several other sacks of gold, and placed a heavy flat rock on top of it. Dora estimated there were several thousand dollars worth of gold buried in the hole.

By the time Dora cleaned the dishes from the evening meal, Tucker had crawled into his blankets and was fast asleep. As he fell into a deep slumber, Dora considered sneaking away, believing she would have a head start of several miles by the time her husband awoke in the morning. Dora rejected, and then revised, her plan several times that night. She was worried that, once out on the trail, she would be set upon by wild animals or Indians. Ultimately, she decided that none of the hazards she might encounter during her escape could be worse than the hell that came with living with Clem Tucker.

Around midnight, Dora slipped quietly from the tent and made her way to one of the mules. After bridling and saddling it, she quietly led it away from the camp for about ten minutes before mounting. Praying that the sound of the animal's shod hooves on the rock would not wake her husband, Dora rode slowly down the mountain trail and out onto the plains.

For the rest of the night, Dora followed the seldom-used trail in the light of the waning moon. When the sun rose in the morning she was a harried and nervous wreck and on the verge of a breakdown. Throughout the night every sound she heard terrified her—birds chirping, squirrels rustling among the branches of the trees, wind stirring the leaves.

Dora hoped to encounter a ranch or some travelers, any-one who might provide succor. It was not to be, but the greater the distance she placed between herself and Sheep Mountain, the more her spirits rose. Freedom for Dora never felt so good.

The feeling did not last long. Around mid-morning the mule went lame and was unable to carry her. She turned it loose and proceeded on foot for another three or four hours. Tired, hungry, and thirsty, Dora stumbled into a copse of trees near the side of the trail where she found a spring. After slaking her thirst with the cold water, she laid down in the grass and fell asleep immediately.

Late in the afternoon, a noise stirred Dora from her deep sleep. Groggily, she sat up and looked around. Only a few feet away and drinking from the spring was Tucker. Looking up, he smiled at her and approached. As she tried to rise, he kicked her hard, knocking her back to the ground. With that, he pounced on her and beat her with his fists until he thought she might be dead.

But Dora wasn't dead. Still lying in the grass, she regained consciousness around sundown and heard the sounds of Tucker setting up camp. Feigning sleep, she watched her husband through slitted eyes as he cooked a meal over the campfire. Just beyond the fire and near the spring, she spotted his mule, loaded down with the flour sacks containing all the gold Tucker had taken from his new mine. As Dora watched, Tucker unloaded the gold from the mule and stacked it next to his bedroll. After checking on the mule, Tucker finally crawled into his bedroll and fell asleep.

For what seemed like hours, Dora stared at the sleeping man. She was afraid to move, afraid any sound at all would awake him and send him at her once again, beating her like he did before. Presently she rose up on one elbow and paused for a long time, watching the prone form. He did not move, and the sound of his snores reached her ears.

Confident her husband was deep in sleep, Dora rose to her feet and quietly, very slowly made her way over to Tucker's rifle, which was leaning against a rock near the spring. A few moments later, Dora placed the end of the barrel against the head of the sleeping Tucker, pulled the trigger, and blew his head apart.

The sound of the rifle frightened the mule which ran away into the night. Dora threw the rifle down, turned, and began running down the trail. As she forged ahead, she believed was going insane from the terrors of the previous twelve hours.

Three days later, Dora wandered into a camp of Ute Indians. She feared she had survived the horrors of Clem Tucker only to be killed by Indians. The Utes, however, proved to be friendly. They fed her, treated her blistered feet and sunburned skin, and, after placing her on a horse, escorted her to Golden and left her near the edge of town.

Some Golden citizens spotted Dora walking into town. Her disheveled appearance and filthy clothes immediately attracted the attention of some townsfolk, who in turn alerted church officials who eventually took Dora in and cared for her. Despite the ministrations of caring individuals, no one could get Dora to speak a word. They came to believe she was a mute. Eventually, Dora came to trust a woman named Sarah Gibson, who looked in on her from time to time. Gibson happened to be the wife of the editor of the town's newspaper. Presently, Dora told Gibson the entire story of her series of ordeals, beginning with the death of her first husband, her marriage to Clem Tucker, the journey to Sheep Mountain, the discovery of the gold mine, her escape, and the subsequent killing of Tucker.

Sarah Gibson related the tale to her husband who was fascinated by the account of the strange woman. He was determined to serialize the story of Dora's experiences, and as a prelude to that undertaking, organized an expedition to Sheep Mountain in an attempt to find Tucker's gold mine. Using the directions provided by Dora, editor Gibson led a party of men to Sheep Mountain. After arriving, they searched the region for three weeks without finding anything. They eventually returned to Golden and Gibson immediately sought out Dora in order to obtain more detailed directions.

It was too late. By this time Dora Tucker, a somewhat fragile woman to begin with, finally succumbed to her cumulative ordeals and plunged into the depths of insanity, barely able to communicate.

Gibson made at least one more attempt at finding the gold mine at Sheep Mountain, but again returned empty-handed. The years rolled by and Dora Tucker finally passed away in an asylum in Denver. The few people who knew about Clem Tucker's Sheep Mountain gold mine eventually forgot all about it.

In 1896, two Colorado prospectors were on their way to Sheep Mountain to try their luck at prospecting when they stopped to make camp near a spring in a copse of trees located out on the plain just to the northeast of the peak. As one of the men busied himself with gathering firewood, he discovered a skeleton. Lying next to the skeleton was a very old and rusted rifle. When the prospector examined the skull, he noted that it appeared to have been blown apart by a large caliber rifle, most likely the rifle that lay beside it. Little did he know that he was looking at the skull of the late Clem Tucker, and that somewhere nearby were several sacks of gold he had carried from his Sheep Mountain mine. With the passage of so many years, it is likely the canvas had rotted and only piles of gold-laden quartz remained somewhere in the tall grass.

The next morning as the prospectors broke camp, one of them found one such piece of gold-filled quartz, and a cursory search of the area yielded about a half-dozen more. The two men presumed the gold had likely fallen from the ore sack of a previous camper, or perhaps from the pockets of the dead man, and that there was little chance of finding much more of it. An hour later the two rode away, leaving behind somewhere in the grass an incredible fortune in gold.

In 1901, Durango resident W. C. Fallon was seated in the back yard of his home enjoying the calm of a summer afternoon when he saw a snake drop out of a tree and land on the roof of his house. As Fallon watched, the snake crawled into the attic through a roof vent. Bemoaning the interruption, Fallon decided he needed to find the snake and get it out of the house.

Fallon had been in the attic of the house only once before, and that was several years earlier when he purchased it from the previous owner. The former occupants left some old trunks, broken furniture, and stacks of newspapers and magazines.

After searching for the snake for about an hour, Fallon decided to take a break. He sat back against an old chest, pulled one of the old newspapers from an adjacent stack, and began reading it. On the front page was an article about a woman named Dora Tucker who killed her abusive husband and left his body somewhere in the foothills of Sheep Mountain. The article went on to tell of the late husband's discovery of a rich gold mine in the mountain, a mine that apparently yielded several ore sacks of fine gold, and one that has not been found since his death. Intrigued, W. C. Fallon decided to conduct a search for the mine himself.

For the next twenty years, Fallon made dozens of trips to Sheep Mountain in search of Tucker's old mine. He never found it, but he maintained a detailed journal of his searches. When Fallon died in 1931, the journal came into the possession of his son, George. After reading the journal, George Fallon was convinced that the mine existed and that it was now up to him to find it. For the next ten years, George Fallon visited Sheep Mountain over and over again in search of the gold mine. From time to time, the younger Fallon found small amounts of gold, but Tucker's mine eluded him just as it did his father. In 1941, George Fallon made his last trip to Sheep Mountain and finally, reluctantly, gave up the search.

The story of Clem Tucker's Sheep Mountain gold would likely be a very minor, even forgotten, one were it not for a significant event that occurred in 1989. Two weekend hikers returned home to Denver from Sheep Mountain with their pockets filled with quartz. They showed some friends the crystals, explaining that they found them in an old abandoned mine in a seldom visited canyon. When the two were informed that the quartz contained gold, a very rich gold, they were surprised and delighted. They immediately planned a return trip to Sheep Mountain.

For two weeks, the two men searched across Sheep Mountain but were unable to relocate the canyon with the old mine shaft. Frustrated, they gave up, but planned to return again at the first opportunity.

The story of the lost mine and the gold-laced quartz found by the two hikers made the rounds, and soon Sheep Mountain was crawling with prospectors and treasure hunters. For the time being, however, Clem Tucker's gold mine, in spite of luring dozens of hopeful searchers to the mountain, remains lost.

In addition, somewhere out on the plain along the old trail that once led to Sheep Mountain from the northeast lies what remains of the several sacks of gold left there by Tucker. In a grove of trees near a spring, by now scattered about the ground, are what Dora Tucker claimed were several thousand dollars worth of gold taken from Clem Tucker's mine, gold that was left there after Dora killed her husband and fled into the night.

BURIED SHIRLEY GANG HOLDUP LOOT

In the extensive and colorful history of Colorado outlaws, Jim Shirley was only a minor figure. Nevertheless, he figured prominently in a payroll heist and the subsequent caching of a quantity of gold and silver coins estimated to be worth many thousands of dollars at today's values.

In the late summer of 1896, Shirley and his gang—comprised of George Law and another man known only as Kid—held up the Prosser, Conkling, and Company quartz mill near Central City and escaped with a $10,000 payroll in gold and silver coin.

From Central City, the bandits fled southwestward into the mountains and for several weeks evaded the posse they knew was certainly following them. Gradually, they made their way to the small mining town of Animas Forks in San Juan County and approximately twelve miles northeast of Silverton. Somewhere just on the outskirts of Animas Forks, Shirley and his men buried the payroll, intending to return for it in a few months when the excitement about the robbery had died down.

For the next two days, the outlaws visited the tiny settlement of Animas Forks but always returned to their camp near the foot of the mountain where they buried the payroll. In spite of the late summer season, the temperatures were close to freezing at these high altitudes and the outlaws were ill-prepared for the cold weather.

One afternoon as the men sat around a campfire drinking coffee and trying to stay warm, they spotted a posse riding toward them. Taking cover among the nearby trees, they fired their guns at the approaching lawmen. The outlaws, clearly outnumbered and out-armed, but also suffering the discomfort of the biting cold, surrendered to the lawmen in a short time and were taken back into Animas Forks where they were locked up. Despite repeated interrogation, the three men refused to reveal where they buried the payroll.

Law enforcement throughout this part of Colorado during this time could best be described as informal. Rather than setting a trial date for the accused outlaws, the lawmen simply told the outlaws that if they did not reveal the hiding place of the quartz mill payroll, they would be hanged in the morning. The three prisoners were left to think about their plight in the old and drafty wooden building that served as a jail cell in Animas Forks.

When the sun went down that evening, the temperatures dropped significantly, and the night grew bitterly cold. The three prisoners huddled together in a fruitless attempt to keep warm. When this proved to be insufficient, they decided to become active to try to ward off the below freezing temperatures—they decided to see if they could find a way to escape. About two hours before dawn, they managed to pry loose some of the boards at floor level, squirmed their way out of the jail, and fled into the night.

Several weeks later on the morning of 13 October 1896, Jim Shirley and his two partners surfaced in the town of Meeker in Rio Blanco County in the western part of the state. Riding stolen horses, the three men arrived in town, dismounted, and entered a tavern a short distance away and across the street from the city's bank. For the entire afternoon, they watched the bank from the tavern window and began making plans to rob it.

Around 3:00 pm, Shirley noted that it appeared the bank was preparing to close for the day. Turning toward Law and Kid, he told them it was time. Buttoning their heavy coats, also stolen, against the cold outside, the three outlaws led their horses to the edge of the small town where they tied them to some growing bushes. They then made their way to the bank.

Law and the Kid walked through the front door of the bank as the employees were preparing to close. Shirley went to the rear of the building and entered the back door. When one of the tellers informed Law that it was too late in the day to do business, the outlaw yanked a revolver from his holster, placed the barrel on the cashier's forehead, and pulled the trigger. As the cashier fell dead to the ground, Shirley, who had come up behind the remaining employees, herded them into a corner of the bank building. As Law and the Kid filled canvas sacks with cash and coin, Shirley stood guard by the window.

Law's shot apparently alerted several of the townsfolk to what was happening at the bank. The sudden news that the bank was being robbed spread quickly throughout the small town and within moments citizens, miners, prospectors, and merchants were armed and taking shelter behind barrels and water troughs and inside nearby buildings. All quietly watched the front of the bank, waiting for the outlaws to come out.

Meanwhile, inside the building Shirley, apparently unconcerned with the growing number of armed citizens outside, ordered the employees to unlock the safe. The employees insisted they did not possess the combination of the lock to do so, so the bank manager was dragged from his office and forced at gunpoint to open it. Finally, the heavy door of the safe swung open and the outlaws stepped inside. Here, Shirley filled several cotton sacks with gold dust. When the bags were full, he handed them to the Kid.

Glancing outside the bank window at the two dozen or more armed men who had gathered across the street, Shirley calmly stepped outside and shot H. C. Clark, the owner of the hardware store across the street. As Clark fell to the ground, the rest of the makeshift posse scrambled for better cover just as Shirley suspected they would.

As Shirley and Law ran for their horses at the edge of town, the Kid dropped to one knee and began firing at the angry and armed citizens who were now coming out of their hiding places. As the Kid turned and lept off the boardwalk onto the dirt street in front of the bank, he was cut down by rifle fire, hit by at least five bullets.

Shirley and Law saw the Kid fall as they were climbing into their saddles. Shirley fired his revolver several times into the growing crowd but hit no one. A man shooting a rifle from a rooftop took aim at Shirley, fired, and knocked the outlaw from his horse with a mortal wound to the head. About the same time, Law was shot in the thigh and fell from his horse. Seconds later, townsfolk crowded in around the downed outlaws, guns at the ready should it be necessary to finish them off.

Shirley and the Kid, both dead, were dragged to a local carpenter's house to be fitted for pine caskets. Since there was no physician in Meeker, George Law was carried to the livery stable where he was treated by the blacksmith. After his wound was cleaned and bandaged, Law was taken to the jail and placed on a cot.

After receiving information that the outlaws who

robbed the quartz mill met their match at Meeker, the Central City sheriff traveled to that town to interview the lone survivor. The sheriff, a man named Flood, met with Law in his jail cell and offered him a deal: He told the outlaw that if he told him where the quartz mill payroll was buried he would take him back to Central City and turn him loose. If he refused, he would leave him in the Meeker jail with the promise that the townspeople would surely not be satisfied until they saw him hang for the bank robbery and the killing of the bank teller.

Suffering from a high fever as a result of a serious infection in his wound, Law, in his delirium, provided some directions to the buried payroll loot as well as he could remember. Contrary to his promise, Sheriff Flood, after receiving the directions, left the outlaw to face Meeker justice and simply rode away. It was said he rode directly south to Animas Forks.

On arriving at the approximate location described by Law, Flood was troubled to learn that a recent landslide had covered the area with rock and rubble. Though he poked among the slope for several days, he never found the buried payroll.

Landslides are common in this part of the Rocky Mountains, and it is entirely possible that another one may occur here some day that might just as easily uncover the site where the Shirley Gang buried the quartz mill payroll, now estimated to be worth close to $50,000.

Animas River Valley Gold

Sometime during the mid-1800s, a French-Canadian trapper known only as Pierre left the Canadian Rockies and traveled far to the south into what is now New Mexico. Possessing an intense curiosity to see what lay beyond the next ridge, Pierre spent many leisurely months traveling and trapping throughout much of Montana, Wyoming, and Colorado.

While examining the possibilities of fur trapping along the upper reaches of the Animas River in a canyon located west of the San Juan Mountains in southwestern Colorado, Pierre discovered several abandoned mines. Nearby he found the tumbled-down remains of crude stone residences along with some very old tools and equipment suggestive of long ago Spanish occupation and mining.

On examining one of the nearby open shafts, Pierre was surprised and delighted to find a thick vein of shiny quartz densely laced with pure gold gleaming brightly in the light of his torch.

Excited by his find and by the prospect of becoming wealthy, Pierre decided to travel to the nearest town and purchase some mining equipment. The next morning he broke camp and continued southward into what is now New Mexico and to the closest settlement he knew of.

One week later the French-Canadian arrived in a tiny hamlet in northwestern New Mexico. Here he met Juan Sanchez, a small rancher with a herd of several dozen horses. Pierre and Sanchez grew to be friends and eventually the trapper shared the information pertinent to his discovery of gold. Soon the two men formed a partnership—the rancher would supply horses and laborers and Pierre would lead them to the gold mines.

After several days of planning and preparation, Pierre and Sanchez, along with twenty-six laborers, a like number of horses, and thirty pack mules carrying provisions for several months, left the small village one April morning and proceeded northward toward the Animas River Canyon.

The long trip through the mountainous country was uneventful. Game and water were plentiful, and by the time the party arrived at their destination, men and stock alike were well-fed and watered.

After setting up camp on a flat stretch of grassy flood plain that extended from the river bank, one of the laborers who was cutting wood near a stand of trees suddenly called out. Waving Pierre and Sanchez over to his position, he pointed to a distant ridge on which stood several Indians observing the activities of the newcomers. Pierre immediately identified them at Utes.

The presence of Indians initially created some degree of apprehension among the members of the party, and a heavy guard was posted while the rest of the men worked in the mine. As time passed and the threat of Indian attack never materialized, the guard was relaxed somewhat and the miners gradually became accustomed to the occasional silent and distant presence of the Utes.

Weeks turned into months and the men labored in the mines as much as fourteen hours each day, removing great quantities of the extremely rich gold that was separated from the crumbly quartz and placed in leather packs. As this incredible wealth accumulated, the numbers of Ute Indians observing from the ridges gradually began to increase, but still made no attempt to approach the camp.

During the first week of November the miners began to run low on provisions. In addition, Pierre became concerned about the approaching winter and the possibility of heavy snows isolating them in the canyon and making the hunting of game difficult. By now they had accumulated enough gold—sixty leather packs full—to load all of the pack mules, and the French-Canadian decided it would be prudent to break camp and return to New Mexico, taking their ore with them. Pierre intended to convert the gold into cash, pay off the laborers, split the remainder with Sanchez, and, since the gold content of the shafts appeared inexhaustible, finance a new expedition to return to the canyon the following year.

Two days later, the party of miners rode out of their campground, herding the gold-laden pack train along before them. Just as they departed, a heavy snow began to fall which made travel difficult. After proceeding only a few miles in the worsening storm, Pierre ordered a halt near some hot springs which emanated from a steep red cliff. Here, he told the men, they would wait for the worst part of the storm to pass before continuing. The gold was unloaded from the horses and mules and the stock were turned loose in a nearby meadow to seek grass through the deepening layer of snow. The men, after preparing a sparse meal, huddled under blankets in a vain attempt to keep warm.

The following morning as the fog lifted from the river

valley, it was discovered that all of the horses and mules were missing. Pierre immediately dispatched a half dozen men to search for them, but when they had not returned two hours later he grew concerned and concluded that Indians had taken the mounts and killed the searchers.

Fearful of remaining in the area, but now unable to transport the heavy gold, Pierre ordered a wide shallow hole dug near the base of the cliff. Into this hole the gold was deposited, and once all of the gold-filled packs were placed in the excavation, it was refilled and covered with rocks and tree limbs.

Taking what food and arms they could carry, the remaining twenty-two men divided into four groups and left the canyon, each traveling in a different direction in order to confuse the Indians. They agreed to meet at Sanchez' ranch.

Several weeks later Pierre, Sanchez, and two others finally arrived at the ranch. Frost-bitten, weary, and starved, it took several weeks for the men to recover from their difficult journey. Though Pierre and Sanchez remained at the ranch for several months, none of the other miners were ever seen again and it was presumed the Utes had overtaken and killed them.

It was not long after recovering from his escape that Juan Sanchez was killed, his neck broken as a result of being thrown from a horse. Pierre himself never fully recovered from his ordeal; he lost several toes as a result of frostbite and had great difficulty walking. Though he often expressed a desire to return to the hot springs near the red cliffs region of the Animas River Valley to retrieve the hidden cache of gold, he remained afraid of the Indians and said he would not make the journey until he could organize a large, well-armed force of men to accompany him.

As time passed and Pierre grew older, his enthusiasm for returning to Colorado to recover the gold dimmed. An old man in 1899, he finally realized he would never see his fortune again.

Pierre made a friend in a young Mexican named Pedro Giron. One day, the old French-Canadian told Pedro of the rich gold mines in Colorado, the caching of sixty leather sacks full of gold ore, and the harrowing escape from the Indians. As well as he could remember them, Pierre provided Pedro with directions to the mines, pertinent landmarks, and a description of the site where the gold was cached.

Giron, in the company of three other men, made a trip to the Animas River Valley a year later. Using Pierre's directions, he found what he believed was the meadow in which the party camped while they mined the gold. Giron even found items that had been left in the camp by the miners as well as evidence of a large scale separation process where the gold had been removed from the quartz. The mines, he discovered, had been covered up by a landslide that apparently struck the area only about a year earlier.

Traveling downstream, Giron decided to try to locate the immense cache of gold. Though he found the red cliffs and the hot springs, old Pierre's description of the site was vague and confusing. In addition, a narrow gauge railroad had recently been constructed in the canyon and much of the topography had been rearranged in altering the gradient to accommodate the tracks.

Giron returned immediately to the small village where Pierre lived in the hope of obtaining more precise directions, but was saddened to discover the old man had died during his absence.

Giron made several more trips to the canyon over the

next few years. On one occasion he believed he had located the site of the cache, but was forced to travel to the nearest settlement to obtain equipment and provisions. During the return trip to the canyon, Giron's mare slipped on a slope of loose gravel, falling on her rider and crushing his leg. The injury was very serious and it took Giron several months to recover. When he was finally able to leave his bed and hobble around on crutches, he came to realize like Pierre before him that he would never be able to return to the Animas River Valley again.

The gold, sixty leather sacks of it, is still buried in a shallow hole near the base of some red cliffs in the Animas River Valley. Nearby flow a series of small hot springs, the gurgling water offering an accompaniment to the wild birdsongs echoing throughout the canyon.

CHIMNEY ROCK GOLD

During the autumn of 1852, a small party of men wound their way through a multitude of passes in the Rocky Mountains. Five in all, they rode horseback and led a pack train of seven mules—two of the mules carried supplies and the remaining five transported just over 700 pounds of gold ingots.

For many weeks the five men traveled, thus since departing the gold fields of California during the late spring. It is known they were bound for Santa Fe, but beyond that point their destination remains a mystery. Ultimately, four of them did not survive the trip. Who they were is also a mystery, save for one man—Sam Carven.

Carven and his four companions were extremely weary from the long hours and the many weeks on the trail. They were anxious to cross the Rocky Mountains and reach the plains where travel would be easier and where they were certain to find a settlement in which to rest for several days. They were growing irritable with the monotony of their long journey, and from time to time bickered among themselves. The only thing that kept them together was the incredible wealth they carried with them, wealth that was intended to provide each of the five men with a life of luxury on returning to their homes.

Of the five, Carven was the only one who bathed and shaved when the opportunity presented itself—the other four had neither bathed nor groomed themselves since leaving California and as a result looked unkempt and shaggy. In addition to the irritability generated by the endless days of tiresome travel, game had been scarce and the five had not eaten fresh meat for more than a week, not since crossing the Animas River near the present-day town of Durango.

As they ascended a slope in the Ignacio Mountains in western Archuleta County, they unexpectedly rode up to a poor Indian camp. Approximately fifty yards ahead of them and just off the trail, four or five tepees could be seen clustered around a central fire. Meat was cooking on a spit and the aroma tantalized the men. They decided to ride into the camp and see if the Indians would invite them to share a meal.

Their approach, though friendly, was not perceived as such. As the five riders neared the tepees, they noticed there were no men in camp, only women and children who immediately ran into the woods at sighting the newcomers. Reining up their mounts in the middle of the camp, they called for the Indians to return, but all remained hidden in the brush.

With no one around to barter with for the meat, the five men began helping themselves, eventually sating their hunger. After resting for a short time following the meal, they decided it was time to move on. As Carven approached his mount, the horse spooked and ran headlong into a nearby tepee, tumbling it to the ground and into the campfire. As the tepee caught fire and burned, the five rode away, their seven pack mules trailing behind them.

Later that day as they rode down the eastern slope of the Ignacio Mountains, the five men paralleled a stream. In the distance, they noted an odd rock formation composed of tall, somewhat slender columns jutting skyward from a low hill. They eventually came to another stream believed to be the Piedra River. Along both sides of the river were level meadows of lush grass, perfect for grazing. Since the horses and mules had not enjoyed such rich fare for many days, the tired travelers decided this would be a good place to set up camp for a few days and take a break from the weary pace they endured.

As the travelers were preparing their evening meal in their new camp, the men of the small tribe frightened by them earlier in the day returned from a hunting trip. As soon as they arrived in the camp, the women and children came running from their hiding places and told of being attacked by the intruders. Pointing to the burnt tepee, they told the warriors that the whites ate all of the meat that was cooking and tried to destroy the camp. The warriors, growing increasingly angry, decided to go in pursuit of the five white men and exact revenge.

As two of the whites prepared dinner in their campsite several miles away, the other three unloaded saddles from the horses and the gold from the mules. The animals were then led some distance from the camp to the lush grasses and staked out for the night. The gold-filled packs were dragged to the campsite and stacked next to the fire.

The following morning, the sun was barely up in the sky when the five men groggily stumbled from their tents to face the day. During the night, the Indians, Utes, had crept to a position some one hundred yards away and took cover behind rocks and trees near where the white men's horses and mules had been staked. There they waited for the opportune moment to strike.

After cutting the stake ropes, the Indians, yelling and brandishing bows, arrows, and spears, drove the animals straight into the camp. Carven, who had gone into the trees on the other side of the camp to empty his bladder, heard the noise and sprinted toward a dense cover of brush about fifty yards away. Halfway to the hiding place, he hit his shin against a rock outcrop and fell, losing his pistol in the process. Crawling the rest of the way, Carven reached a place of concealment, and from it he watched as his companions were cut down by the vengeance-minded Indians.

The sudden attack caught the white men unaware, unprepared, and defenseless. Within minutes it was over and the four men in camp were dead, each punctured by dozens of arrows. After killing the whites, the Indians set about rounding up the horses and mules. Apparently they were unaware of the fifth member of the party, for no attempt was made to look for Carven.

After gathering the horses, the Indians poked through the camp gear, taking some items for themselves. When they chanced upon the sacks filled with gold ingots, they were puzzled. The Indians had no use for gold or any other precious metal save for ornaments, and were generally dismayed by the attraction it held for the white men. One by one, the Utes picked up the sacks, carried them approximately one hundred feet away to a shallow ravine that fed into the Piedra River, and dropped them in.

One of the Indians, who was interviewed many years later about the incident, said over the years the water that flowed down the little ravine backed dirt up against, and eventually over, the sacks of gold, effectively covering them all. At the time of his interview, which was in the

1880s, he claimed the gold was still there, as he passed by it from time to time while out on hunting trips.

Carven silently watched from hiding as the Indians dumped the gold in the ravine. While they were occupied with scavenging items from the now completely destroyed camp, Carven quietly crawled away. When he thought it was safe to do so, he finally got to his feet and ran down the mountain slope toward the east, ever hopeful of finding succor at a nearby village or ranch. Months later, with the help of strangers he encountered along the way, he finally made it to Santa Fe, New Mexico.

Carven remained in Santa Fe for many years, afraid to return to the mountains to attempt to retrieve the gold, afraid of facing the Utes. As time passed, and as peace was gradually restored to Colorado and the Indians were placed on reservations, Carven finally decided it would be safe to return. Now, he thought, the 700 pounds of gold would all belong to him.

Carven made his way back into the region in 1890 and took a job on a ranch owned by a man named Cooper. When he was not working, Carven rode throughout the countryside trying to locate the chimney rock formations and, eventually, the gold that had been thrown into the nearby ravine.

One evening during roundup when Carven, Cooper, and a number of other cowhands were seated around the evening campfire smoking cigarettes, Carven told the story of the journey from California, the attack by the Indians, and the 700 pounds of gold.

At the end of the tale, one of the cowhands spoke up and said he knew that particular rock formation well, that it was called Chimney Rock, that it was located not more than twenty miles from where they now sat, and that it was close to the confluence of the Piedra River and Stollsteimer Creek.

Several days later, Carven told Cooper he wanted to ride over to Chimney Rock to see if he could locate the gold and asked Cooper to accompany him. Cooper declined, stating that he had too much work to do to go riding off into the mountains.

Carven was gone for two days. When he returned to the Cooper ranch he told the owner that he had found Chimney Rock and, a short time later, the old campsite where his companions were killed. He even found the rock outcrop on which he banged his shin. He explored up and down several small ravines not far from the campsite, but could not remember exactly which one the gold was thrown into. After digging into some of them and finding nothing, he returned to the ranch.

Subsequent trips to the Chimney Rock campsite like-wise yielded nothing, but Carven remained certain that he was close to the gold, that it was just a matter of locating the correct ravine and digging in the right place.

Months passed, and Carven was still unable to relocate the gold. Eventually, he told Cooper he was giving up and returning to New Mexico. He drew his pay and the next day he was gone, never to be heard from again.

In later years, Cooper himself even tried searching for the lost gold, but after several unsuccessful trips to the Chimney Rock area he, like Carven, finally gave up.

It appears likely that seven hundred pounds of gold still lie in a shallow ravine not far from Chimney Rock. At today's values it would amount to well over three million dollars.

THE CURSE OF SLATE MOUNTAIN

One afternoon of a late summer day in 1849, a party of some thirteen horsemen arrived at the small settlement of Glenwood Springs in Garfield County. The riders, as well as their mounts, appeared exhausted from many long days on the trail. After placing their animals in a local livery, the men sought hot meals and hotel rooms.

During the next few days, Glenwood Springs residents became acquainted with the leader of the party, a man named Buck Rogers, and learned the group was headed for the California gold fields with high hopes of striking it rich and returning to their homes in Illinois as wealthy men.

Several days later after the horses were sufficiently rested and the men had replenished their supplies, the party set out once again, continuing westward. Though different versions of this tale exist, it is believed that at the end of the second day of travel out of Glenwood Springs, the thirteen men stopped to camp at a location they referred to as "the base of Slate Mountain."

The next morning, one of the men rose early and climbed along the slopes of Slate Mountain. He found what he believed were promising indications of gold on the mountain. Excited, he returned to camp to deliver the good news.

By the time breakfast was finished, the party of men broke into open disagreement. Rogers and four others insisted they remain at Slate Mountain and mine the gold they already found. The remaining eight men wanted to push on to California and try their luck in the already established gold fields there. Finally, an agreement was made, the gear and provisions divided, and the eight dissenters, bidding their companions goodbye, rode away to the west.

Rogers and his friends set to work immediately, and much to their delight were retrieving gold from the mountainside at a steady rate. By the time the first snows of autumn started falling, they had already amassed what they estimated to be approximately $100,000 worth of fine gold ore.

Not wishing to become trapped in the deep snows that occur in this part of the state with no provisions, the five men decided to send someone back to Glenwood Springs to purchase supplies. Rogers was elected, and taking approximately $500 of gold dust, rode out of camp leading two pack horses.

On arriving at Glenwood Springs, Rogers was easily tempted by the lure of the town's saloons. Thinking it would do little harm, he treated himself to a whiskey. The first one seemed so tasty after working those long hours on the mountain that he decided to have another, then another, and another. Rogers' first night of drinking led to several more, and before he sobered up he realized he had spent almost a week in town, had purchased no supplies, and had spent most of the gold dust. To add to his problems, three feet of snow that fell on his final night in town covered the landscape as far as the eye could see.

Consumed by guilt, Rogers used the balance of the gold to purchase a small amount of supplies, loaded them onto the pack horses, and headed back to Slate Mountain. When he was approximately two miles from the campsite, he noted that the snows were much heavier here, and he soon found himself trailing through five foot high drifts.

When he finally arrived in camp, he encountered a tragedy. While he was in town drinking himself into a stupor, the heavy snows on Slate Mountain had generated an avalanche that roared down the mountainside, killed his four companions, and obliterated all traces of their mining operation.

Saddened by the loss of his friends and overwhelmed by guilt from his conviction that he was somehow to blame, Rogers returned to Glenwood Springs where he took up residence. He continued drinking heavily and soon gained a reputation as the town drunk. For the price of a drink, Rogers would relate the story of the gold discovery on Slate Mountain and the loss of his friends. When asked for directions to Slate Mountain, Rogers remained vague and elusive.

What became of Rogers is not known. Some say he died in Glenwood Springs not many years later and was buried in a pauper's grave. Others maintain he tried to return to Illinois and perished along the way, a victim of consumption.

In 1881, a stranger arrived in Denver, took a room in a fine hotel, and paid for it in gold. That same evening, he went to a local tavern and bought drinks for the house, again paying in gold. During the course of the evening the stranger became quite inebriated and made friends with the bartender. When the bartender asked him about the origin of the gold he was spending so freely, the newcomer

said it came from a place the locals referred to as Slate
Mountain, and that it was located several miles west of
Glenwood Springs.

After a full evening of drinking, the stranger confessed
to the bartender that he, along with a partner, found the
gold on Slate Mountain, but that they got into an argument over how to split the gold. During the course of the
quarrel, the stranger bashed in the head of his partner
with a heavy rock, killing him instantly. The stranger told
the bartender that he was spooked by the killing and was
afraid to return to the mountain and dig for more gold. In
his drunken stupor, the stranger gave the bartender directions to the gold deposit at Slate Mountain.

The following morning, the bartender awoke with a
splitting headache. He walked a few blocks to the office of
the town's only physician, complaining of severe pain,
dizziness, and nausea. Before evening, he was delirious
and had to strapped into a bed. When he regained some
semblance of consciousness, the doctor told him he did not
have long to live. The bartender died the next morning, but
before he did he provided the doctor the directions to the
gold mine at Slate mountain.

The following day, the miner who had given the directions to the bartender boarded a stagecoach bound for the
east. Several miles out of town, the coach turned over and
rolled down an embankment, killing two of the passengers, one of which was the miner.

Weeks later, the doctor, unmindful of the fact that at
least six people who had a connection to the gold mine on
Slate Mountain were dead, decided to go look for it himself. When he was able to get away from his practice, the
doctor searched for the Slate Mountain gold for several
years without discovery or incident. During conversations
with friends, the doctor revealed that the bartender told

him the gold was not far below the timberline on the mountain. Beyond that, he told them very little.

During the summer of 1886, the doctor traveled alone to Slate Mountain to search once again for the elusive gold. When he did not return at the expected time, his oldest son led a search party out to look for him. They finally found him, dead. He was apparently on his way back to Denver when his horse spooked and threw him to the ground, breaking his neck. Not far away they retrieved his horse and discovered the leather saddle packs were filled with gold!

In 1889, an old man traveling afoot walked into the stagecoach station at Red Cliff, Colorado, some sixty miles east of Glenwood Springs as the crow flies. Station manager A. H. Fulford welcomed the old man, noticed his ragged clothes and worn out boots, treated him to a free meal, and invited him to spend the night by the warm fire.

During the course of the evening, the old man told Fulford he was a miner and that he had found an extremely promising outcrop of gold on what some people called Slate Mountain out west of Glenwood Springs. Fulford, who was familiar with the story of Buck Rogers and his bad luck at Slate Mountain, was keenly interested and asked many questions, Finally, the old miner pulled some ore samples from his pack and showed them to Fulford. The station manager, who had once been a prospector and miner himself, recognized the high quality of the gold.

Throughout most of the evening the two men talked about the discovery of the gold, and before retiring for the night, they agreed to become partners, hire some workers, return to Slate Mountain, and mine the gold.

The next morning, Fulford told the old miner it would take a few days to make the necessary arrangements to make the trip back to Slate Mountain. In the meantime, he gave the old man some money and told him to go to town and have a good time. It turned out to be bad advice.

After three or four strong whiskeys, the old miner grew belligerent with other patrons in the bar, cursing and picking fights. It was not long before he goaded one of the patrons into a brawl, and before it was over, the old man lay dying on the barroom floor, bleeding copiously from a knife wound in the chest.

When Fulford was informed of the incident, he rushed into town to see about the old man, but he was already dead. He died without providing Fulford complete directions to the gold on Slate Mountain.

Undaunted by the lack of information concerning the exact location of the gold and seduced by the promise of finding great wealth, Fulford turned the stage station over to a helper, outfitted himself, and traveled to Slate Mountain. Alone, he wandered the flanks and slopes of the mountain for weeks without finding anything. Refusing to give up, he remained in his crude camp near the base of the mountain even as the first heavy snows of late autumn were falling.

He was seen in Glenwood Springs the day after Christmas. He came to town to purchase supplies and told acquaintances he felt like he was on the verge of discovering the outcrop of gold that had been found by the old miner and by Buck Rogers before him.

Fulford was never seen alive again. Late the following spring, a pair of hunters found his body on the flanks of the mountain. Like Rogers' companions forty years earlier, he had been killed by an avalanche. Among Fulford's belongings they found approximately seven pounds of high grade gold ore!

By now, area residents were talking about the curse of Slate Mountain. Several who might otherwise have been tempted to search the mountain for the gold were now discouraged by the presumed curse.

To further confuse the issue of the gold on Slate Mountain, few who have studied this tale can agree on exactly which mountain carried that name during the mid to late 1800s. More than one mountain in this region has been called Slate Mountain in the past.

Should the real Slate Mountain be discovered, the one where the Rogers party and others found gold, the enterprising searcher for the ore will have to contend with what many believe is a strong curse, one that is responsible for the deaths of at least nine people.

THE GOLDEN JESUS

Somewhere in southwestern Colorado, crammed into a dusty cliffside niche partially walled up with rocks, lies one of the greatest treasures in the history of North America. The treasure is a single item—a statue of the Christ child—and it is cast from almost pure gold. It is believed the statue stood approximately three to three-and-a-half feet tall and was nearly perfect in its proportions. The statue, called the Golden Jesus, was so heavy that a special wagon had to be built to carry it. Its great weight, ironically, was the reason it had to be abandoned.

If found today, the Golden Jesus would be worth uncountable millions of dollars.

* * *

One late spring day sometime during the 1770s, a company of Spaniards arrived at the New Mexico village of Santa Fe. Among the group of men were soldiers, blacksmiths, cooks, laborers, and miners. The newcomers were welcomed to the village by one Padre Escalante, a Catholic priest who had already made a reputation for himself with his hundreds, if not thousands, of successful conversions of the area Indians.

The Spaniards, relying on very old maps, were on their

way to some point many miles to the north and west of Santa Fe. There, they told Padre Escalante, they expected to find several rich deposits of gold that had been worked many years earlier by some of the first Spaniards ever to enter this country. A number of different versions of this part of the legend exist: One has the Spaniards heading to and finally arriving at the La Sal or the Henry Mountains in southeastern Utah; another version, the one most commonly accepted by researchers, is that the location was somewhere in present-day southeastern Colorado, most likely the La Plata Mountains.

Padre Escalante told the Spaniards he was in the process of preparing for a journey through that very region of Colorado and offered to lead them. He warned them, however, that the Indians who lived in that area were extremely hostile to newcomers and he suggested to his countrymen that they be on their guard at all times. Several days later, with equipment and provisions tied securely to packhorses and mules, Padre Escalante offered a blessing over the voyagers into the far, remote region and gave a prayer for success. Little could he have known what a great success the mining operation would turn out to be. And little could he foresee the terrible tragedy that was to eventually befall the Spaniards.

On finally arriving at the La Plata Mountains in southwestern Colorado, the Spaniards, along with Padre Escalante and his contingent, established a camp and for several days rested the travel-weary men and animals. Approximately one week later, Escalante bid his countrymen goodbye and, assembling his charges, set out for points farther north.

It was only a short time later when the Spaniards located the old diggings for which they sought. They immediately bent to the task of reopening several of the abandoned shafts, and before long the rich ore was being dug from the rock matrix with impressive consistency. The gold-filled quartz was soon being transported down the mountainside by burros and laborers to one of several arrastres. Here, the ore was removed from the crushed rock and carried to the nearby crude smelter where it was melted down, poured into molds, and fashioned into ingots. Soon, a large quantity of the gold bars had accumulated.

As the mid- to late-autumn storms and snows arrived in the La Plata Mountains, the leaders of the Spanish expedition began making plans to travel to Santa Fe where they intended to spend the winter. When the spring thaw arrived the following year, they planned to return to the mountains and resume their mining activities.

As the men were preparing to shut down the mines for the winter, disagreements arose over how to divide the gold. The disagreements quickly turned bitter and occasionally violent, Finally, one of the leaders made a proposal that appeared to satisfy all: He suggested that each man be provided a small share of the gold to take to Santa Fe to spend as he saw fit. The remainder of the gold was to be cast into one large form and transported to the authorities in Mexico City. All eventually agreed to this proposal, and it was finally decided to cast the gold into a statue bearing the likeness of the child Jesus in honor of Padre Escalante. A mold was skillfully prepared from large pieces of pumice found nearby, and within the week the statue was completed. The statue was named "Jesus del Oro," or "The Golden Jesus," by the miners.

Because of the incredibly great weight of the Golden Jesus—it has been estimated that it weighed several hundred pounds—a special wagon had to be constructed. With great difficulty the Spaniards loaded the statue onto the wagon and negotiated the narrow, winding trail down from the mountains that eventually joined the road to Santa Fe.

Traveling with the Golden Jesus was so slow that the

party barely covered ten miles the first day. On several occasions, they were forced to stop and make repairs on or modifications to the wagon. Rather than delay the entire company because of the extremely slow rate of progress, the leaders of the expedition directed approximately half their number to proceed on to Santa Fe, while the rest would remain to guard the Golden Jesus and catch up later.

Dividing their numbers proved to be a costly decision. Though the Spaniards occasionally spotted Indians watching them as they went about their mining activities during the previous months, direct encounters were few and far between and open confrontation never occurred. It appeared to the Spaniards that the Indians were only curious about their activities in the mountains and posed no serious threat. The Indians, on the other hand, were merely biding their time and waiting to strike at the most opportune moment.

Now, with the forces of the Spaniards divided, that time had come. On the morning after half of the contingent rode ahead to Santa Fe, the Indians struck. As the Spaniards crawled from their bedrolls and went about the task of preparing breakfast, the Indians fired a barrage of arrows into their midst from behind nearby rocks and trees, killing several at this first volley. Those that survived scrambled for their weapons, and after priming their blunderbusses began to return fire.

Though the Spaniards possessed a firepower of a greater technological level than the Indians, they were too few and too inept with warfare to provide much resistance. The surprise attack had taken its toll, and the priming and reloading of the clumsy blunderbusses allowed the aggressive attackers to pick off their enemy one by one.

During the battle, one of the ranking officers gathered four of the Spanish soldiers together and assigned them

the duty of escaping with the Golden Jesus. Quickly hitch-
ing the four-mule team to the stout wagon, the four men
needed little incentive to flee from what would surely be a
massacre. Two of the men positioned themselves in the
wagon seat, and the other two rode alongside the vehicle
astride their own mounts. Away from the battle they fled,
the wagon straining beneath the heavy load of the Golden
Jesus.

The Indians watched the four depart and let them go.
The majority of the hated Spaniards remained and would
prove to be easy to kill.

As the sounds of the battle faded in the distance, the
four Spaniards fleeing with the Golden Jesus quickly discerned the folly of this venture. It soon became clear that
the wagon could not withstand the tortures of the rocky,
bumpy trail without coming apart. After they had traveled
no more than four miles, the soldiers decided to find a
place to hide the Golden Jesus, a place safe from the
Indians, but one to which they could easily return to
retrieve the statue.

Within minutes they found such a place. While legend
holds that the Golden Jesus was hidden in a cave, most
who have researched this particular tale are convinced it
was likely a deep, wide niche they found in the side of a
bluff. Since most of the exposed rock in this area is of an
igneous intrusive nature, true caves, in fact, are not common here at all.

After dumping the heavy statue from the wagon bed
onto the ground, the four Spaniards, using long poles
hastily cut from nearby trees, levered it over to and into
the niche, shoving it as far to the rear of the opening as
possible. After placing the Golden Jesus inside the niche,
they quickly walled up the front with rocks they found
nearby. Believing the Golden Jesus to be secure until such
time as they could return, the four Spaniards continued on

to Santa Fe, arriving safely several days later where they reported the attack by the Indians.

Aware of the savage and ferocious nature of the Indians to the north and west, the Santa Feans were reluctant to become involved with an expedition to travel into the La Plata Mountains to investigate the outcome of the Indian attack and to retrieve the Golden Jesus. It was only after much pleading and making promises of huge rewards that the four Spaniards finally assembled a party of men to return with them.

It was several weeks later when the contingent of some twenty men, all well-mounted and well-armed, set out toward the northwest. Many days later they passed the place where the Golden Jesus had been hidden. The four Spaniards wanted to see first to their fellows, convinced there were no survivors and promising to provide each of them with a Christian burial.

Their fears were soon realized. In a short time they came upon the remains of their companions. None of the Spaniards survived, and all had been scalped and mutilated almost beyond recognition. It was a somber group that spent most of the rest of the day digging graves and burying the men.

Camp was made nearby for the night. The next morning as the men finished their breakfast and began packing their gear, they were surprised by the sudden appearance of Indians riding toward them from out of the forest. Savage yells were accompanied by a fusillade of arrows and lances. Panicked, the Santa Feans climbed into their saddles and, for the most part, undertook an unplanned and disorganized retreat back down the trail. Three of their number were killed with the first volley of arrows, and the remainder, having just seen what it was like to fall into the hands of the Indians, whipped their mounts as hard as they could in hope of saving their own lives. As they rode past the location where the Golden Jesus was cached, the four Spaniards who were part of the original party knew they would likely never be able to return to this area to recover it.

At this point, the legend is difficult to pin down. There are several versions of subsequent unsuccessful forays into the foothills of the La Plata Mountains to try to locate and retrieve the Golden Jesus. Likewise, there are at least four versions of what became of the four Spaniards who survived the Indian attack: One claims they refused to ever return to the La Plata Mountains; another states they left the country and returned to their Spanish homeland; another maintains they returned to Mexico; yet another suggest they did, in fact, return to the mountains to find the statue and were killed by Indians during the attempt.

In addition, there is the version of this amazing tale that involves a curse.

Somehow, with the telling and retelling of the legend of the Golden Jesus, a curse has become attached to it. Most of the scholarly folk who research and study tales of lost mines and buried treasures generally don't believe in curses, but enough bizarre happenings have been attached to the legend of the Golden Jesus to make one wonder if, indeed, such a thing could be true. In fact, some researchers believe that the Spaniards themselves, the ones who actually made the Golden Jesus, were the first victims of the curse, falling beneath the furious attack by the Indians.

According to one story, an old prospector who allegedly found the lost Golden Jesus ultimately died as a result of his discovery.

In 1873, a wagon train consisting of people from Illinois and Indiana traveling to California was winding along a trail through southwestern Colorado not far from the present-day town of Hesperus when they chanced upon an old man lying near the side of the road. At first, they thought the old fellow was dead, but on closer inspection found him to be emaciated, dehydrated, blind, and near death. Not far away grazed a saddled horse and a well-packed burro.

After placing the old man in one of the wagons and getting him to drink some water and take some broth, the travelers marveled at the incredible story he subsequently related.

He was prospecting, he said, some distance away in the La Plata Mountains and had set up camp just off an old, little used trail in the shade of an overhanging canyon wall. One late afternoon as he relaxed in camp, his eyes wandered to the base of the wall and noticed what he took to be a niche, or a narrow horizontal crack, that appeared to have been walled up by someone using nearby rocks. Curious, he walked over to the niche and began pulling away the rocks.

Once he had removed enough rocks to allow sunlight to penetrate the interior, the prospector was stunned to find himself gazing upon a statue of what appeared to be the child Jesus. He tried to pull the statue out of the enclosure but it was so heavy he was unable to budge it. Examining the statue more closely, the old man was even more surprised to discover it was made from almost pure gold!

Later that evening as the old man sat around his campfire, he considered ways to remove the statue from its present location and transport it to Denver where he hoped to convert it to cash. As he pondered such things, he was suddenly seized by an odd sensation, one that caused his body to stiffen. One moment he was sitting on a rock drinking coffee, the next he lay unconscious, not to recover until sometime in the morning. When he finally regained consciousness, the sun was at least two hours in the sky. On trying to rise from the ground, the first thing the old prospector noticed was that he was almost blind. He was able to discern the differences between light and shadow, but beyond that he was virtually sightless.

The prospector somehow managed to gather up his horse and burro and pack most of his equipment. After placing the animals on the trail that led down from the mountains, he gave them their lead and hoped they would carry him to succor. It was late afternoon of the second day of traveling in this manner that he was found by the members of the wagon train.

The old man moved into and out of delirium for two days after telling his story and then finally died. Another victim, some maintain, of the curse of the Golden Jesus.

At least one other encounter with the mysterious golden statue has been reported. Two men from Tucson, Arizona—Adrian Connor and Gus Grijalva—followed the La Plata River to some point close to its source in the La Plata Mountains. Over the years, the two men had heard stories of lost gold and silver mines in the area, as well of tales of placer mines where one could pan impressive quantities of gold from the area streams. They thought they would try their luck here, but all they found was death.

On their third day in these mountains, the two men were examining quartz outcrops in some of the exposed granite along an old trail that wound through the foothills of the range. They turned their horses out to graze on a small grassy meadow and hiked along the base of a canyon wall. At one point, they encountered a low opening in the wall, a kind of narrow, horizontal niche about twenty feet long and only four feet high at its widest. Portions of the niche appeared to have had rocks stacked in front of it, but in the center most of the rocks had either fallen away or been pulled out by someone. Peering inside, the two saw nothing but a large hump in the center of the floor of the niche. Climbing inside, they brushed some of the accumulated dust and dirt from the object and were amazed to discover it was a statue. Later, one of them was to describe the statue as having been cast in the image of the Christ child and claimed it was made from pure gold!

With great difficulty, the two men pulled and shoved the statue to the edge of the niche, but it soon became clear they would not be able to move it much farther without some help. They soon hit upon the idea of constructing a skid on which they intended to place the statue and drag it to some location with their horses where they could procure a wagon stout enough to transport it.

During the next two hours, a number of logs were lashed together to form a crude sled which was carried to the mouth of the niche. The men intended to use the horses to pull the heavy statue out of the niche and onto the skid. While Grijalva tied ropes around the statue, Connor went to get the horses which were grazing nearby. After bridling both and saddling one, Conner mounted the animal and grabbed the reins of the other. As he turned the horse he was riding toward the niche, the animal suddenly bolted, throwing Connor from the saddle. On hitting the ground, Connor broke his neck.

Grijalva witnessed the accident from where he was standing near the niche and immediately jumped up and ran to his fallen companion. When he reached Connor he saw that his friend was still alive but in great pain. Grijalva tried to move the injured man, but even the slightest touch proved excruciatingly painful. He had no choice but to make his friend comfortable and ride to the nearest town for help.

After saddling the second horse, Grijalva rode toward Durango, some twenty-five miles by winding trails to the

southeast. Durango was the only settlement in the area
large enough to support a physician. After two hours of
alternate hard riding and some walking, Grijavla's mount
weakened and finally stumbled and fell to the ground,
throwing the rider. After rising, the horse limped badly
and it was clear it would not be able to continue the journey. Grijalva broke his left arm in the fall. Painfully, he
rose to his feet, quickly assayed the situation, and proceeded at once to walk toward Durango.

Two days later Grijalva was found by two cowhands. He
had been wandering aimlessly along the bank of a small
tributary to the La Plata River when the riders spotted
him. As the cowhands approached, Grijalva began screaming in fright, warning them to stay away, and muttering
something about a Golden Jesus. After calming the
stranger down, one of the cowhands got him to climb up
behind him on his horse. About one hour later, they delivered him to the ranch house. The next morning, the rancher loaded Grijalva into a wagon and had him taken to
Durango.

At Durango, a doctor was forced to amputate Grijalva's
arm at the shoulder because of the severe infection that
had set in. In the days that followed, the patient babbled
incessantly and incoherently about his friend Connor and
about a golden statue bearing the likeness of the Christ
child. Listening carefully to the man's ramblings, the doctor eventually learned that Grijalva's partner lay somewhere in the La Plata Mountains with a broken neck. He
immediately alerted the town marshal.

Two days later, a rescue party found Connor's body. It
was not known how long he remained alive after Grijalva
left, but there was little left of him now—he had been partially consumed by wild animals.

In their concern over wrapping the body in a blanket,
tying it to a horse, and returning to Durango as soon as

possible, the members of the rescue party failed to notice the open niche and partially exposed statue of the Golden Jesus some distance back down the trail.

As far as anyone knows, the Golden Jesus is still lying there in the niche where it was originally placed by the four Spaniards who were fleeing from the attacking Indians. The location is apparently somewhat remote and rarely visited save for perhaps weekend prospectors, hikers, and maybe some hunters. According to the history, it is also near an old trail, one that is seldom, if ever, used anymore.

It is difficult to impossible to determine how much the golden statue weighs, but if it is cast of almost pure gold and if it took four men with pole levers to place it into the niche, then it must be considerable. Retrieving it will take several people and/or heavy equipment.

If found today, the value of the Golden Jesus, both in terms of its gold content as well as its historical significance, is inestimable.

LOST HANSEN MINE
IN MOFFAT COUNTY

Moffat County, Colorado, has never been associated with the great gold and silver strikes like much of the rest of the state has, but somewhere in the western part of that county near the Utah line lies a small, but apparently once very productive, gold mine that has eluded searchers for well over a century. That the gold exists has never been doubted—it has been seen by several people—but the location of its origin remains a mystery to this day.

* * *

Red and Eli Hansen were prospectors who arrived in northwestern Colorado from Minnesota sometime during the 1870s. Preferring solitude to crowds, the two men eschewed the densely mined regions of the northern and southern Rocky Mountain regions of Colorado, preferring instead to try their luck in some of the more remote areas, far from the disturbance and company of others. Most of their activity kept them in what is now Moffat County, the northeasternmost county in the state of Colorado.

From time to time the Hansen brothers would arrive at a small settlement in the region, sometimes in Colorado and sometimes in neighboring Utah. Here, they would stock up on provisions and always pay in gold dust or gold nuggets. The two brothers were always asked about their mining activities, but they generally replied that, while they were finding a bit of color here and there, they were yet to make the big strike they were hoping for. The miserly and careful manner in which they counted out their meager amount of dust led the proprietors of the mercantile houses to believe their modest claims. The brothers were an amiable pair and got along well with everyone they met in the towns. Red Hansen was distinguished by his flaming red hair that could be seen a mile away. Younger brother Eli was very blond and slight of build.

One afternoon, the Hansen brothers rode into the town of Jensen just across the border in Utah. The two men were in high spirits as they roamed through the mercantile selecting a number of items to purchase. When presented with the total, the brothers smiled at the proprietor and gleefully paid for the goods with large gold nuggets which they poured from a cloth ore sack. The proprietor was impressed with the quality of the gold, and even more impressed with the quantity of nuggets remaining in the sack. When he asked the brothers about their strike, they replied that they had finally hit it big at their mine located several miles away to the east, vaguely pointing toward the direction from which they just arrived.

For the first time in their lives, the Hansen brothers paid for a room in a nearby inn instead of camping just outside of town. That evening, they treated themselves to a fine dinner and liquor. By the time they retired to their beds for the evening, news of their gold strike had circulated throughout the small community of Jensen.

The next morning as the Hansen brothers loaded their goods onto packhorses, they were observed by individuals who remained hidden behind closed doors and behind buildings. Later, when the two men rode out of town, they were followed by a party of some five or six men who trailed along approximately two miles behind them.

When the brothers stopped for lunch, Red Hansen saw the mounted riders watching them from a distance and became suspicious when they didn't ride any closer. About two hours later when the brothers resumed their journey, they discovered they were being followed. Concerned that the men behind them were intent on locating their gold mine or perhaps robbing them, Red and Eli Hansen left the trail and rode along a somewhat winding, circuitous route through some low foothills. The going was rough, but it provided the brothers an opportunity to elude the men behind them. By the end of the day, they had managed to outdistance and evade their trackers. Secure that they were no longer being trailed, the brothers camped under a rock ledge that night and departed for their mine the following morning.

Two-and-a-half months later, the Hansen brothers found it necessary to return to Jensen for more supplies. After placing a quantity of gold nuggets into a sack—just enough, they determined, to pay for their goods—they set out on the trail toward town.

For two days they traveled across the countryside, enjoying the sights and pausing occasionally to hunt wild game for a meal. On the third day as they were riding through Pool Canyon, the brothers were approximately fifteen miles from Jensen when they noticed a half-dozen riders approaching them on the trail. The riders were coming fast and hard and had their guns drawn.

When they came within twenty yards of the Hansens, the newcomers opened fire, killing the two men at the first volley. No sooner had the two miners hit the ground than

the riders were searching through their victims' pockets
and packs. Presently, one of the men found the ore sack
containing the gold to be used for purchases in town.
Cursing at what they considered to be a small amount of
gold, the bandits rifled though the dead men's gear, taking
guns, ammunition, and even their boots. Finally, they
dragged the bodies approximately sixty yards off the trail,
placed them under an overhang of a low cliff, and covered
them with rock, dirt, and debris. Following this, the six
men rode back to Jensen where they spent the gold on a
minor drinking spree at one of the town's taverns.

It was claimed a few of the Jensen townsfolk recognized
items in the possession of the six men they were convinced
belonged to the Hansen brothers, but their fear of the bandits inhibited them from doing or saying anything. The
next morning the six men rode away, never to be seen in
the area again. Likewise, the Hansen brothers were never
seen again either, at least not alive.

From time to time, a few of the residents of Jensen
would ride across the line into Colorado in search of the
Hansen brothers' gold mine, but having no precise directions to go by whatsoever, they were never successful.

Several years later, an area rancher named Harry Chew
told of a discovery he made while looking for some stray
cattle in Pool Canyon. Riding along a rock ledge, he spotted what he thought was an odd-shaped rock lying
beneath it. On closer investigation, he discovered it was a
human skull. After digging through a nearby pile of rock
and dirt, Chew eventually uncovered a second skull and
two complete skeletons. Still clinging to the head of the
second skull was a lock of flaming red hair. Chew suddenly realized he had found the remains of the Hansen brothers.

Months after his discovery, Chew followed the trail out

of the Colorado end of Pool Canyon in hopes of finding the Hansen brothers mine, but he never did.

* * *

About two years after rancher Chew found the bodies of the Hansen brothers, an old Indian arrived in Jensen on foot walking from the east. He came to town, he said, to purchase some goods. After filling a sack with the Indian's selections, the proprietor of the store informed him of the total purchase price and was promptly handed a sack of gold. After counting out the required amount and returning the rest, the proprietor inquired about the origin of the gold. The Indian replied it came from the Hansen brothers old mine!

When pressed for details, the old Indian claimed he lived near the location of the mine when the Hansen brothers first opened it and that he often visited with them while they were working. The Indian would occasionally bring the brothers wild game he shot or trapped, and in turn the brothers often invited the Indian to dine with them. Eventually they became good friends.

When the Hansen brothers traveled to Jensen on what was to be their last days alive, the Indian accompanied them. On the final day of travel, however, the Indian remained in camp to clean up while the brothers rode into town. Since Indians were not particularly welcome in Jensen in those days, he intended to wait on the outskirts of the town for the return of the Hansen brothers. As the Indian was riding to catch up to the two men, he heard gunshots, and from a place of concealment watched as a group of highwaymen killed the Hansens, searched the bodies and the packs, and then dragged the two dead men over to the cliff and covered them with rocks. Fearing he would be accused of the killings if he went into town, the Indian simply returned to his home in the mountains.

When the proprietor pressed the Indian for details concerning the location of the Hansen brothers gold mine, he remained silent. Finally, he shouldered his load of goods and walked out of town back toward the Colorado line. He was never seen in Jensen again.

The portion of Moffat County to the east of Pool Canyon is rugged, remote, and sparsely populated. It is entirely possible a gold mine, or several gold mines for that matter, could exist in this region without anyone knowing their location, since it is hardly visited by humans. Somewhere in this vast expanse of mountains and canyons lies the lost gold mine of the Hansen Brothers.

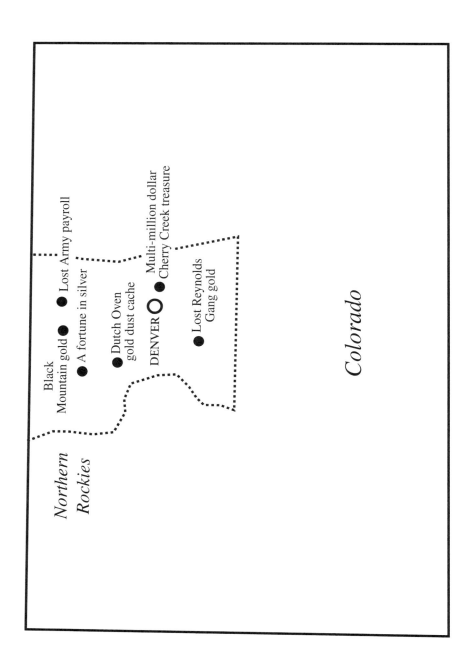

Black
Mountain gold ●

● Lost Army payroll

● A fortune in silver

● Dutch Oven
gold dust cache

DENVER ○

Multi-million dollar
● Cherry Creek treasure

● Lost Reynolds
Gang gold

*Northern
Rockies*

Colorado

THE NORTHERN ROCKIES

The Rocky Mountains of Northern Colorado are testimony to untold geological violence and upheaval that has taken place here during the previous several million years.

To explore and examine this part of Colorado is to view a landscape shattered and shaped by numerous episodes of volcanic activity, both above ground and below. Dozens, if not hundreds, of dead or dormant volcanos dot the surface, the spaces between them often filled with the products of volcanic eruption—lava beds and ash deposits. At other times, and deep below the surface, fiery hot magma under intense pressures invaded the crevices, bedding planes, and faults of the fractured crust, forcing tongues and fingers of molten material into these spaces. Here, the magma, now far from its source, slowly cooled and formed dikes and sills of igneous intrusive rock. Here and there where the conditions are just right, gold, silver, and other metals were formed in some of these pockets.

For eons prior to this amazing volcanic activity, and for ages afterward, this landscape, under great tectonic stress as a result of the continental plates pushing and compressing against one another, forced uplifting, folding, and fracturing of the brittle rock crust, slowly yet inexorably pushing the earthquake-ridden igneous, sedimentary, and metamorphic rock thousands of feet high into altitudes where the temperature rarely drops below freezing.

In these frigid, high-altitude environments, glaciers formed from the accumulation and compaction of snow, sometimes growing to hundreds of feet in thickness. Pulled downslope by gravity, these formidable masses of ice ground their way slowly downward, abrading, plucking and otherwise eroding the rock of the mountains, sculpting it, shaping it, wearing it down, and leaving behind a myriad of landforms including tors, aretes, cirques, tarns, and glacial troughs, all of which provide this particular landscape with the shapes and textures for which it is known today.

Into this environment arrived early Native Americans who took up residence. Here they found game and water in abundance along with territories they felt comfortable defending against neighboring tribes.

By the time early explorers arrived in Colorado's northern Rockies, the area was populated, in places, by several different tribes of Indians. Initially, encounters were few and, with some exceptions, not particularly violent. Then gold and silver were discovered. To mine and extract the precious ore, newcomers were often forced to trespass into Indian territory. Confrontation was inevitable, and cultural violence became all too common.

The results were inevitable. Outnumbered and out-armed, the Indians were doomed to defeat and removal from their homelands, thus opening this part of the Rockies to even more miners and settlers. Soon, the mines generated settlements, many of which evolved into towns. A few of these towns, of course, eventually grew into great cities. Indeed, much of the history of Colorado is tied to mining, and much of this mining was related to the extraction of gold and silver.

Today, the Northern Rockies of Colorado are associated with many things: Skiing, tourism, fishing, hunting, hiking, and backpacking, just a few of an endless number of outdoor activities to be found here. Few people realize that the picturesque setting for these activities is comprised of the rock and crust that was once subjected to incredibly violent geologic forces and once considered the richest in the world in terms of the gold and silver found there.

Many of the old mines are still there. Some were ultimately exhausted and closed down. During the early stages of mining in this area, the threat of Indian hostilities caused many miners to simply leave or be killed. Others, still containing gold and silver, were simply abandoned for a variety of reasons. Many of these mines are chronicled, the records easily found in county courthouses. Others, including some that were very rich and productive but were never formally filed on are simply lost.

In addition, it has been estimated gold and silver worth many millions of dollars yet to be discovered still resides in and on this rock: New discoveries are announced every year; new placer mines are opened; new veins of ore are encountered during prospecting ventures into the wilderness.

Indeed, the northern Rockies are rich, not only in ore but in the tales and the legends.

LOST REYNOLDS GANG GOLD

Among the annals of famous Colorado outlaws, the Reynolds Gang is given some deserved recognition. Jim and John Reynolds had a history of petty thievery, were responsible, it is believed, for some murders, and were generally run out of nearly every town they ever visited. The brothers, along with other members of the gang, met their end in August 1864 following the robbery of the Fairplay-Denver stagecoach at the 10,000-foot high Kenosha Pass.

Numerous versions exist of the Reynolds Gang robbery and the subsequent hiding of the stagecoach loot. Intensive research over the years since the robbery, however, has winnowed out most of the questionable aspects of the event, leaving the following compelling tale.

* * *

On the morning of July 31, 1864, the Fairplay-Denver stagecoach was making a scheduled run. As the six horses strained to pull the coach up the steep incline toward Kenosha Pass, the driver and the guard spotted a group of men riding toward them. Believing them to be travelers, the two waved a greeting. Moments later as the mounted party neared, the driver and guard were stunned to see they were wearing masks and holding revolvers in their hands. Jim Reynolds, who referred to himself as "Jim the Bold," nudged his horse up close to the stagecoach and ordered the guard to throw down the strongbox. He did so, and mere seconds after it hit the ground, the outlaws had broken it open and were scooping up almost $65,000 worth of currency and gold dust.

Reynolds then told the driver to continue on to Denver, and as the stage rumbled away toward the northeast, the outlaws, nine in all, rode away into the trees. Sometime later, they came to the North Fork of the South Platte River and followed it downstream until they reached Elk Creek, a tributary. They then followed Elk Creek into the foothills of Mount Logan near the present day boundary between Gilpin and Park counties and set up camp not far from the headwaters.

Concerned that lawmen might be ranging about the countryside looking for them, Jim Reynolds told the members of the gang that they would hide out near Mount Logan for a few days before heading out again. As the men were setting up camp, cutting firewood, and cooking the evening meal, several posses were indeed following the gang's tracks and closing in on the Elk Creek campsite.

The posse closest to the Reynolds gang was led by General David Crook, chief of government investigators in Colorado, and it was composed primarily of volunteers made up of irate miners and prospectors, men who had grown tired of depredations by the Reynolds Gang and men who had been impacted by the recent robbery of the stagecoach.

Jim and John Reynolds removed two pokes of gold dust to be divided among the outlaws. The rest, they said, was to be buried and retrieved at a later date. The brothers transported the stagecoach loot to a location in the foothills of the mountain approximately midway between Elk Creek and Deer Creek, which flowed out of adjacent canyons to the west. The site selected by Jim Reynolds was an old, long-abandoned mine shaft. Just inside the entrance to the shaft, Reynolds scooped out a shallow hole, placed the gold and currency within, and then covered it over. Jim Reynolds then jabbed his hunting knife into a nearby dead tree, placing it such that the handle pointed toward the treasure cache. Some versions of this tale have the knife handle pointing toward the grave of one of the gang members, but this notion has long since been discarded.

That same evening following dinner, Jim Reynolds advised the rest of the gang that in order to avoid capture, they must move their campsite to Geneva Gulch about one mile to the west beyond Deer and Elk creeks. The following morning, he told them, they would depart the area individually and meet some weeks later at a predetermined location in the Greenhorn Mountains.

On arriving at the Geneva Gulch location late the following afternoon, the outlaws were busy preparing dinner when they were surprised by the sound of hoofbeats rapidly approaching the camp. Looking up, they spotted General Crook's band of volunteers riding down on them with guns blazing. One of the outlaws, a man named Singletary, was killed immediately and two others suffered slight wounds. Not having enough time to retrieve and saddle their horses, the gang members fled on foot through the trees.

The next morning, all but John Reynolds and another outlaw named Jack Stowe were captured by Crook's volunteers

The captured outlaws were treated roughly—beaten,

tied, and thrown into the back of a wagon and transported to Denver where they were charged with robbing the Fairplay-Denver stagecoach. It did not take a jury long to find the outlaws guilty and sentence them to jail terms at Fort Leavenworth, Kansas.

Three days after leaving Denver, the prison wagon transporting the convicted robbers to Kansas was pulled to a stop along the side of the highway and the prisoners were ordered to step out of the coach. Marched to the edge of a nearby field, they were made to stand side by side. Seconds later, they were all shot to death and left to lie where they fell. The bodies were found several days later.

During the last week of August, lawmen who had been searching for John Reynolds and Jack Stowe picked up the trail of the two outlaws and followed it through the settlements of South Park and Two Buttes near the Arkansas River. There, the trail vanished and the posse finally gave up and returned home.

Several weeks later, the two outlaws showed up in Santa Fe, New Mexico. They had been in town for no more than two days when Stowe got into a fight and was shot dead.

Within weeks after the death of Stowe, Reynolds partnered up with another outlaw named Al Brown. Together, and for the next few years, the two men conducted a number of robberies in New Mexico. During this time, Reynolds went by the alias of Will Wallace.

The depredations by Reynolds and Brown soon gained the attention of area lawmen. Constantly pursued, Reynolds and Brown eventually left New Mexico and traveled to Denver. Along the way, they stopped in Taos to steal some fresh horses from a ranch. They were spotted in the act by cowhands who fired upon them. Reynolds was shot in the stomach but, along with Brown, managed to escape.

When they were convinced they were finally safe from pursuit, the two men made camp and examined Reynolds' wound. It was clear the outlaw was not going to survive.

Knowing he was going to die, Reynolds gave Brown directions to the location where the Fairplay-Denver stagecoach loot was buried. He told him to ride a short distance above Geneva Gulch to a point where one of the outlaw's horses got mired in a bog and had to be abandoned. Near the head of the gulch, Reynolds said, he should turn to the right and go along the foothills until reaching the headwaters of Deer Creek. At this point, one can look up toward the timberline and see an old mine shaft and tailings. The loot was cached in a shallow hole hastily scooped out just inside the entrance. Not far away, Reynolds told Brown, can be found a dead tree with a knife sticking out of it, the handle pointing toward the shaft. As he related the directions to Brown, Reynolds sketched a map on a piece of paper with the lead tip of a bullet.

Brown had never been to the Mount Logan area, but he knew someone who had. He quickly enlisted the help of Jim Cochran, who agreed to serve as a guide. Days later, the two men entered the region and soon found themselves riding up Geneva Gulch. Near the headwaters of the gulch, they located the bones of the mired horse just as Reynolds described. From there they traveled past Deer Creek but were disappointed to discover a forest fire had burned down hundreds of trees a year or two earlier. Furthermore, it appeared as though a recent landslide had occurred, obliterating any evidence of an old mine shaft on the side of the mountain. Despite searching the region for several days, Brown found neither the tree with the knife stuck in it nor an opening to a mine shaft. A second trip to the area the following year likewise yielded no sign of the cache, and Brown finally gave up the search.

In 1933, a man named Vernon Crow was searching for and found some old mining claims near Handcart Creek, a small stream located a short distance west of Geneva Gulch. He remained camped in the area for several days while he pursued his investigations. One morning while hiking near Deer Creek, he spied an old rusted knife sticking out of a dead tree. Well aware of the story of the buried Reynolds Gang loot, Crow searched the area for the entrance to the mine shaft but found no sign of it. Before leaving, he removed the knife from the tree.

The lost Reynolds Gang loot is one of the best documented tales of buried treasure in the state of Colorado, and there is little question among researchers that the currency and gold is still buried where John and Jim Reynolds originally cached it. In fact, many believe that the Reynolds Gang loot is the most searched-for lost treasure in the state of Colorado. Unfortunately for the searchers, landslides and forest fires have modified the landscape in this area such that it makes the search extremely difficult.

Regardless of these obstacles, dozens of treasure hunters come to this part of Mount Logan every year, each one hoping to find the cache. Perhaps someday someone will.

LOST ARMY PAYROLL CACHE

Somewhere in Larimer County near the top of a mountain located northwest of Fort Collins and almost to the Wyoming border lies a long lost army payroll cache that, according to researchers, is likely worth an incredible fortune. This cache, or at least a portion of it, was hidden in 1872 and actually rediscovered in 1883. The finder, unfortunately, was killed a short time later and precise knowledge of the location died with him.

* * *

One early morning during the second week of June 1872, $62,000 worth of gold coins was loaded into a military transport coach at the Clark and Gruber Mining Company in Denver. The gold was destined for a military payday at Fort Laramie several days travel to the north.

The wagon driver, George Pritchett, was accompanied by a guard named LeBlanc. As Pritchett steered the mule-drawn wagon away from the loading dock, he was joined by an armed and mounted contingent of the United States Seventh Dragoons which had received orders to escort the payroll wagon to Fort Collins, located some sixty miles to the north. The members of the dragoon patrol, led by Sergeant C. Foster, were armed with .44 caliber repeating rifles as well as revolvers.

The uneventful journey to Fort Collins took two days. On arriving at the military post, Sergeant Foster informed Pritchett that from this point on they would be escorted by a patrol of troopers stationed at the fort. The dragoons bid Pritchett and LeBlanc goodbye and left for the return trip to Denver. The following morning as Pritchett and LeBlanc readied the wagon for the remainder of the trip to Laramie, they were informed that because all available troops were pursuing and skirmishing with warring Ute Indians, no escort would be provided. Colonel Oscar Critchell, commanding officer of the fort, strongly recommended that the departure of the wagon be delayed until such time as the troopers returned from action.

Pritchett, annoyed by Critchell's position, told the colonel that he was inclined to proceed without an escort. Pritchett had never missed a deadline and saw no reason to miss this one. Once again, Critchell emphasized that the payroll wagon should remain at Fort Collins until such time as escort troops would become available.

Pritchett told Critchell that if the wagon made the rest of the journey without an armed escort, anyone they encountered along the way would not be inclined to suspect they were carrying anything valuable and would likely leave them alone. Critchell agreed with the driver's logic, relaxed his stand on the matter somewhat, and allowed the men to drive the wagon out the gate and onto the road leading to Fort Laramie.

Nearly an hour out of Fort Collins, the payroll wagon slowed slightly as it proceeded up a grade toward Coyote Pass not far from the present-day town of Livermore. Near the top of the grade and lurking behind some rocks were four men, rifles at the ready and all eagerly anticipating the arrival of the wagon.

The four consisted of Jeff Borrell and his sons Cobe, Floyd, and Vance. Since his arrival in this part of Colorado several years earlier, Borrell had undertaken several unsuccessful attempts at ranching and other enterprises but failed at all of them. He eventually turned to outlawry and found robbing travelers and stagecoaches and stealing livestock from area ranches was much easier and more profitable than herding cattle. Though never proven, it was also suspected that the Borrell gang was responsible for as many as five murders.

Several days earlier while hanging around the settlement that had sprung up around Fort Collins, the elder Borrell learned about the unescorted payroll wagon and decided it would be easy to rob.

As Pritchett was whipping the mules to the top of Coyote Pass, the Borrells rode out from behind their places of concealment firing at him and LeBlanc. Both men were killed immediately, their bodies tumbling from the wagon onto the dusty road. The mules, startled by the sudden burst of gunfire, broke into a run and were not contained until they had exhausted themselves nearly two miles down the road.

When the Borrells finally overtook the wagon, they climbed aboard, located the strongbox containing the payroll gold, and tossed it onto the ground. After several attempts, the lock was finally shot off. Inside the strongbox were a number of canvas money sacks, each containing gold coins. The four men divided the sacks and stuffed them into their saddlebags. Leaving the mules hitched to the wagon, the four outlaws turned and rode away along a game trail, finally disappearing into the trees and boulders into the higher elevations of a nearby mountain.

It wasn't long after the payroll wagon had rolled out of Fort Collins that it was reported to Colonel Critchell that several troopers had just returned from a scouting patrol. Critchell immediately ordered Lieutenant David Sparks to assemble a platoon consisting of twelve men to catch up to the payroll wagon and escort it into Fort Laramie. Approximately two hours after the departure of the payroll wagon, Sparks and the troopers were already riding up the trail with the intention of overtaking it.

A little more than an hour after leaving the fort, the soldiers found the bodies of Pritchett and LeBlanc. Lt. Sparks ordered four of his men to transport the two dead men back to Fort Collins. With the remaining troopers, Sparks continued following the tracks of the payroll wagon. Several minutes later they found it and the mules in a grove of trees just off the road. Nearby, one of the soldiers found the opened strongbox.

After casting about for clues, one of the troopers located the tracks of the fleeing robbers where they rode up a narrow game trail into the higher elevations of an adjacent mountain. Without hesitation, the soldiers followed.

As Sparks and the soldiers spurred their mounts up the trail, it soon became clear that the U.S. Army horses were not up to the task of the steep climb up the mountain. Little more than halfway to the top, they clearly lacked the stamina to continue. Dismounting, the soldiers tied off their mounts and, carrying their rifles, proceeded on foot.

On nearing the summit, the troopers lost the trail of the outlaws. After scouting a portion of the mountain for over two hours, Lt. Sparks finally ordered a return to Fort Collins. Little known to the soldiers, the Borrells, barricaded in a shallow cave that had earlier been stocked with provisions, had been watching the troopers since they arrived near the summit. With rifles aimed at the approaching soldiers, the outlaws commanded a prime defensive position with an excellent field of fire should they be discovered and forced into a gun battle. At one point, the soldiers were so close to the Borrells that their conversations could be overheard.

When the troopers finally left the mountain, Jeff Borrell told his sons they would remain at the cave for a few days until things cooled down somewhat. Little did Borrell know that Sparks and a contingent of soldiers would remain encamped not far away at the base of the mountain. Furthermore, while the troopers were setting up camp, Sparks ordered two of them to hurry back to Fort Collins to request that a large force of cavalry be sent to aid in the pursuit and capture of the bandits.

By the time the two troopers had reached the fort, several platoons were returning from action in the field. Within a short time, a force of some forty soldiers was assembled. Just before leaving Fort Collins, Colonel Critchell ordered the troopers not to return until they recovered the payroll and captured or killed those responsible for its theft.

The following morning, one of the Borrell sons spotted a large force of soldiers riding up the trail toward the hideout and quickly informed his father. When Jeff Borrell counted the soldiers and saw that they were all well-armed, he decided it would be most prudent to flee. Quickly, he and his sons buried the stolen payroll at the rear of the shallow cave and then piled rocks atop the cache.

Taking only what they could quickly pack into their saddlebags, the outlaws mounted their horses and started riding toward the opposite side of the mountain and away from the pursuing soldiers. They were spotted the moment they broke clear of the covering timber.

At a command from Sparks, a number of the troopers opened fire on the fleeing bandits. Before the Borrells could reach cover, all four were shot from their horses.

When the soldiers reached the fallen men, they found Jeff Borrell, along with sons Floyd and Vance, dead. Cobe Borrell was severely wounded and barely clung to life. A quick search of the outlaws' saddlebags yielded none of the payroll. While Cobe lay dying on the mountain, Sparks tried to get the youth to reveal where they had hidden the payroll gold. Cobe refused to talk, and within two hours he was dead.

While the bodies of the outlaws were being transported back to Fort Collins, Sparks ordered his men to search the mountain for the payroll. Though they scoured the environs for two full days, they found nothing. Eventually, Sparks ordered his men back to the fort.

Critchell, infuriated at the loss of the payroll and the inability of his soldiers to find it, ordered over 100 troops back to the mountain to search it completely—every ravine, canyon, crest, and slope. For almost two months the mountain was explored but still the payroll gold was never found. Furthermore, there was no one left alive who could tell the soldiers where the gold was buried.

Then, during the summer of 1883, the payroll was discovered, only to be lost again within hours.

Some Larimer County cowhands eventually learned about the lost payroll gold and decided to go search for it at the first opportunity. Arriving at the mountain one morning, four cowboys from a nearby ranch, mounted and carrying a two-day supply of food, began exploring the mountain for possible hiding places. Following lunch, they decided they could cover more area if they split up, so they rode out in different directions.

One of the cowboys, Stacy Wehrer, tired after searching all morning, took shade just within the opening of a shallow cave. Behind him and against the far wall, he noted a strange pile of rocks. The more he regarded the rocks, the more he realized they did not occur there naturally, that they were clearly stacked there by someone. He wondered why.

Crawling to the rear of the cave, Wehrer rolled the rocks away and dug into the newly exposed sandy floor of the cave. There, just inches below the surface, he found several canvas sacks containing the lost army payroll gold. Wehrer removed some of the coins from one of the sacks, placed them in a pocket, and reburied the remainder. He then replaced the rocks atop the cache, mounted his horse, and rode out to meet his companions.

When asked by his friends, Wehrer claimed he had no success in locating the treasure, but there was something about the way he said it that aroused their suspicions. Presently, Wehrer told his companions he was tired of the search and that he was going to return to the ranch. Suspecting that Wehrer had located the lost payroll, his three companions confronted him, accusing him of finding it and holding out on them. With that, Wehrer merely smiled, turned his horse, and rode down the trail. Two of the cowboys pulled their revolvers and fired. Later, they claimed they only wanted to frighten him, but two of their bullets found their mark and Wehrer fell from his horse, dead. When they searched his pockets, they found several gold coins, each dated 1872, the year the Borrell Gang robbed the payroll wagon.

Leaving the body where it lay, the three cowhands spent several hours trying to trace Wehrer's route back up the mountain where he found the coins, but they were unable to locate the cache.

Days later, the three cowhands were arrested and charged in the death of Stacy Wehrer, tried, convicted of murder, and sentenced to prison.

* * *

Somewhere in a shallow cave on a mountain adjacent to Coyote Pass lies buried a fortune in gold coins, the remaining portion of the army payroll taken by the Borrell Brothers well over a century ago. Though searched for many times, it has never been found.

MULTI-MILLION DOLLAR CHERRY CREEK TREASURE

Gold mining, smelting, and marketing were major industries in Colorado during the mid-nineteenth century, ones that employed thousands of workers and made millionaires out of dozens, if not hundreds, of men. The extraction, processing, and transportation of this precious metal involved tons of gold, so it is not surprising that some of it, and quite likely a lot of it, got lost, misplaced, or hidden along the way.

Somewhere near Cherry Creek in Douglas County, and perhaps within the present city limits of Denver, is an incredible fortune in four-leaf-clover-shaped gold slugs. Following an attempted robbery in 1860, the gold was hurriedly tossed into nearby marmot dens by a man who hoped to return for it later. To date, it has never been retrieved.

* * *

Because of the occasional difficulty of obtaining coinage in the western part of the United States during the mid-1800s, gold and silver was often fashioned into homemade coins or other objects which, in turn, were temporarily used as legal tender until such time as a shipment of legal coins arrived from the U.S. Mint in Philadelphia. Eventually, a mint was established in Denver, Colorado, to address this deficiency, but until it was constructed and placed into use, a variety of measures were undertaken to ensure the continuance of trade.

In 1860, a private mint which provided temporary legal tender was in operation in Denver. Clark, Gruber, and Company, one of the largest businesses in Colorado at the time, often subcontracted orders for regional tender to small smelters. In June of that year, Thomas Gavin, along with his wife and two sons, signed a contract with Clark, Gruber, and Company to purchase gold ore and process it into coins of five, ten, and twenty dollar denominations.

Gavin learned that the prices for gold ore were significantly less the farther one traveled from Denver. Because most buyers seldom visited these far-flung locations, and because transportation into Denver was often difficult and very time-consuming, the miners in these outlying and oftentimes remote districts were eager to bargain. Knowing this, and realizing the amount of work involved, Gavin took on two partners to help him and explained his plan to them: They would travel to Pike's Peak, purchase the gold, and return it to his smelter in Denver. Gavin was provided a certain amount of money by Clark, Gruber, and Company to purchase the gold. If they could buy the necessary amount for less than what was provided by the company, the two partners could have the difference as their share.

Gavin's partners were James Bullock and Peter Larkin. Bullock was a well known and respected assayer in Denver. Larkin was a newcomer to Denver whose only means of income, as far as anyone knew, was gambling. Together, Gavin, Bullock, and Larkin, leading four pack horses, made the long trip to Pike's Peak.

Within just a few days after arriving at Pike's Peak, the three men purchased just over 700 pounds of gold ore, all of it brought to them in jars, bottles, cloth sacks, and tin cans. In order to reduce the bulk and make it easier to transport back to Denver, Gavin decided to set up a crude smelter at their campsite, melt down the gold, and shape it into small ingots which would be easy to pack. As Gavin cast about for something to use as an ingot mold, Larkin brought him a small Indian-made dish in the shape of a four-leaf clover. The dish was made from pumice, about the size of the palm of a man's hand, and would serve nicely as a mold. Gavin, realizing that four-leaf clovers were associated with good luck, liked the idea. Soon, the three men had fashioned 200 four-leaf-clover-shaped three-and-one-half pound gold slugs from the mold.

As a result of their negotiations with the miners, Bullock and Larkin managed to earn a total of $2,000 which they intended to divide. They were excited about making that much money in a comparatively short period of time and were eager to return to Denver to celebrate. On the evening of the day they finished making the slugs, they dined in camp and decided to entertain themselves with a game of poker.

The game began as a friendly diversion, but soon evolved into one accompanied by high wagers and growing tension, with each man betting portions of his share of the profits. In the beginning, Gavin lost a great deal of money, but gradually his luck changed and he started winning regularly. Sometime into the late evening, Bullock had lost all of his share of the profits and Larkin had lost approximately $200. Finally, Gavin stated that the hour was late and suggested they stop playing and get some sleep.

Larkin grew bitter and objected to Gavin's suggestion. Angrily, he argued that he deserved a chance to win his money back. Gavin resisted, reminding him they had to rise early in the morning, pack up, and begin the long trip back to Denver. Larkin refused to capitulate and continued to demand they play for at least one more hour.

Gavin countered Larkin's demand by suggesting the two simply cut the cards, with the holder of the high card taking all of the winnings, thus bringing an end to the matter. Larkin agreed.

Gavin cut first and held up a ten of clubs. Larkin cut next and looked at his card. When he saw that it was a three of hearts, he reddened and angrily threw it to the ground. He then cursed Gavin and stomped off into the nearby brush to sulk for over an hour.

Later that evening as the three men were preparing for bed, Gavin noticed Larkin pass a revolver to Bullock. As he lay in his bedroll, Gavin grew concerned that the two men were planning to kill him and take the gold for themselves. Later, when he was certain Larkin and Bullock were sound asleep, he retrieved his own revolver from his pack and kept it nearby.

In the morning as the three men prepared breakfast, it appeared at first that the tension between Gavin and his partners had lessened. Gavin, however, maintained his suspicions and was convinced his two partners were acting a bit too friendly, perhaps in an attempt to get him to let down his guard. As they packed their gear and loaded the gold onto the pack animals, Gavin noticed Bullock and Larkin whispering to one another, and he grew ever more wary of the two men.

Most of the journey from the Pike's Peak location back to Denver was uneventful, although Gavin did notice Bullock and Larkin engage in quiet conversation from time to time. Their route took them along the valley of Cherry Creek, a few miles east of downtown Denver. Gavin had learned of a recent gold strike in the area and thought he might be able to pick up some more gold at bargain prices here. As they made their way along the narrow trail that paralleled the creek, Larkin was riding in the front of the single-file pack train, leading two pack horses. He was followed by Bullock, also leading two pack horses. Gavin brought up the rear, relatively comfortable that both of his adversaries were in front of him where they could be easily watched.

At one point along the trail, Larkin spurred his horse to greater speed, and in a few minutes increased the distance between himself and the rest of the pack train. Moments later, Larkin and the two pack horses in his charge disappeared around a bend almost fifty yards ahead. Gavin, concerned about Larkin's actions, spurred his own mount in an attempt to catch up. As he trotted past Bullock, he inquired why Larkin had raced ahead. In response, Bullock pulled a revolver from his belt and fired at Gavin, striking him in the shoulder and knocking him out of his saddle.

In great pain, Gavin was attempting to rise when he spotted Bullock dismounting a few yards away and walking toward him, gun in hand. Convinced Bullock was intent on murdering him, Gavin pulled his own weapon and fired point blank into Bullock's heart, killing him instantly. The two remaining pack horses, startled by the shooting, bolted up the trail in the direction Larkin had fled.

Gavin's horse was also frightened by the gunfire and ran away. Luckily, Bullock's mount was unperturbed by the gunfire and stood where it was left, grazing contentedly on some grass growing along the creek bank. Painfully, Gavin climbed into the saddle and set off in pursuit of Larkin.

Several hundred yards up the trail, Gavin spotted Larkin just ahead of him. On hearing the sounds of pursuit, Larkin turned and fired at the approaching Gavin but his shots were wild. Gavin continued riding toward Larkin, who was having trouble controlling the two pack horses.

Larkin shot at Gavin twice more, emptying his revolver. Holding tightly to the packhorses, he found it difficult to reload, and finally, in frustration, threw his weapon to the ground. In an attempt to escape from the oncoming Larkin, he steered his horse into Cherry Creek in an attempt to cross it. It would prove to be his undoing.

Seconds after Larkin's horse entered the creek, it stumbled, spilling its rider from the saddle. Larkin went under water then rose a moment later, sputtering and spitting. As he tried to get his bearings, Gavin arrived at the creek bank, dismounted, and aimed his revolver at Larkin. The two pack horses, in trying to reach the opposite bank, bumped Larkin, knocking him underwater once again. The second time he surfaced, Gavin aimed again and shot him in the chest. His lifeless body floated away with the current and was soon out of sight.

Gavin remounted and went in search of the pack horses. Though he was bleeding heavily from his shoulder wound and the pain was intense, he was determined not to lose the gold. He searched for approximately an hour and eventually found the four pack animals grazing in a meadow, the fortune in gold still strapped to their backs.

It was late afternoon and Gavin still had a long way to travel before reaching Denver. He was growing weak from loss of blood and had difficulty staying in the saddle. He was also growing concerned he might pass out and lose the pack horses, so he looked for a place to hide the gold until such time as he could recover and return for it. As he rode along Cherry Creek, he happened to look up a nearby hill-side and discovered a temporary solution to his problem. There, among the rocks, he saw a number of marmot holes. Marmots, stout-bodied, short-legged furry rodents burrow out dens in the rocky soil along the slopes of much of the Rocky Mountains.

Leading the pack animals up the hillside, he unstrapped the packs, removed the gold slugs, and dropped them into several of the marmot dens. Following this, he carried the packs and the saddles several dozen yards downstream and stuffed them under some rocks. He then turned the pack horses loose and, growing weaker from loss of blood, continued toward Denver.

About two hours later, the sun was almost down when Gavin rode into a small mining camp. The miners, seated around a campfire eating dinner, spotted Gavin and saw that he appeared to be about to fall out of his saddle. They immediately rushed to his aid and carried him to one their tents. While one of the miners cleaned and bandaged his wound, another tried to get him to eat some broth. Moments later, Gavin passed out.

The following morning, one of the miners rode into Denver to fetch a doctor. Yet another day passed before the doctor arrived at the camp. The doctor turned out to be Gavin's personal physician and was accompanied by Gavin's fourteen-year-old son, Tom. After examining the weakened man in the tent, the doctor told Gavin the wound was badly infected and that he had an advanced case of gangrene. Bluntly, he told Gavin he would likely die.

After the doctor left, Gavin pulled his son close to him and haltingly told him the story of the four-leaf clover-shaped gold slugs, the attempted theft, and how he was forced to shoot and kill Bullock and Larkin. He also explained how he dumped all of the gold slugs into the marmot holes somewhere along Cherry Creek and hid the saddle and packs under some rocks not far away. By the next morning, Gavin was dead.

Following Gavin's funeral, officials from Clark, Gruber, and Company met with the family in order to learn what they could about the possibility of recovering their investment. During the meeting, Gavin's son told the officials about his father hiding the gold in some marmot holes somewhere along Cherry Creek.

Ten days later, a Clark, Gruber, and Company-financed search party traveled the length of Cherry Creek in an attempt to locate and retrieve the gold. While Gavin's tale about hiding the slugs was quite detailed, he left out significant directional and locational information. The searchers were amazed to discover hundreds of marmot holes on the rocky hillsides along both sides of the creek. Though they searched many of them, no gold was found. They were also unable to find the saddles and packs Gavin said he hid under some rocks not far from where he stashed the gold. This was the only search organized by Clark, Gruber, and Company. When presented with the negative results, the company decided no further searches were warranted.

When he grew older, Tom Gavin tried to find the hidden gold on several occasions, but the Cherry Creek treasure remained elusive to him and his investors, and he finally gave up.

Sometime during the 1980s, there was a major gun and knife show held in Denver. Included among the speeches and events were dozens of displays and vendors. Each vendor tried to outdo the other as it related to presenting their wares, and gun and knife tables were often festooned with Indian war bonnets, elk and moose antlers, stuffed animals, and curious geological specimens, all designed to attract the attention of potential buyers.

On one table, lying amid several geodes, rifles, and printed material, was a palm-sized four-leaf clover-shaped slug weighing approximately three-and-a-half pounds. It was sometime during the show that the vendor was informed of the fact that the slug was made from almost pure gold. Until then, he assumed it was merely cast lead. When asked where he found it, he said he picked it up off the ground somewhere in the Cherry Creek Valley east of downtown Denver over twenty years earlier. When pressed, the vendor could not recall the precise location.

It has been estimated that if the Gavin hoard of clover-shaped gold slugs were recovered today, it would be worth well in excess of three million dollars!

A FORTUNE IN SILVER

So many of Colorado's tales and legends of lost mines and buried treasures involve gold that some are inclined to forget that silver is as plentiful, if not more so, in the vast Rocky Mountains that transect the state from north to south. Like today, silver was not worth nearly as much as gold during the early mining and settlement days of Colorado, and since many who entered the business of mining were interested in getting rich as quickly as possible, this precious metal was often neglected, overlooked, or simply discarded. Numerous large deposits of silver, however, were located and some of them turned a number of enterprising men into millionaires in a very short time. Like gold, incredible quantities of silver still remain in the mountains, still waiting to be excavated by the patient and persistent individual or company willing to take a chance on locating and opening up some of the old lost and long-abandoned mines.

One such location is the Entre-Mile Mine located near the border of Jackson and Larimer counties in the northern part of the state. In professional mining and treasure hunting circles, it is well known that a fortune in silver remains in this abandoned mine. Reaching it and excavating it, however, presents a significant and near-insurmountable problem.

* * *

During the summer of 1879, three partners—John Lefevre, Alexander Lefevre, and John Moore found a huge deposit of silver along the foothills on the western side of Mt. Richtofen. The vein of silver was uncommonly thick and ran deep into the mountainside. One mining engineer described the deposit of ore as "endless." A subsequent assay showed the ore to be extremely rich.

Excited at the prospect of becoming successful silver mine owners, the three men invested in some mining equipment, hired some laborers, and before long were digging out and processing the rich silver at a staggering rate.

Within just a few months, a representative from an Illinois business firm, on learning of the rich and productive silver deposit, approached Moore and the Lefevre brothers, discussed the potential of the mine, and offered to purchase it for a huge sum of money. The offer was too good to pass up, and the three men readily accepted it, turning what may have been, and possibly still is, the richest silver mine in Colorado over to the new owners. The company named it the Entre-Mile Mine.

A few weeks after the purchase, a steam plant for processing the ore was moved onto the site, temporary housing for mine administrators and laborers was constructed, and a shaft was sunk and shored to a depth of two hundred feet. Not only did the shaft yield great quantities of the rich ore, but along the way, several feeder veins were discovered, each rich with the same high quality silver. Things were beginning to look very bright for the new owners of the new Entre-Mile Mine.

Then trouble began.

Because the Entre-Mile Mine was located so far from

the ore market in Denver, and because the roads between the mining district and the capital city were in such bad shape, shipping the ore became a serious problem. The expenses involved and the amount of time invested in ore shipments sapped the profits of the mine. The owners disagreed on what measures were necessary to increase profits and soon fell into violent disagreements with one another. In addition, it was soon discovered that the actual ore extraction procedures were being mismanaged. On investigation, it was learned that the mine superintendent had no practical mining experience whatsoever and was hired solely because he was the nephew of one of the owners. More bickering ensued.

Not too many more weeks passed before the company fell into deeper and deeper debt and operating funds were almost nonexistent. Laborers had to be laid off, and work in the mine was eventually suspended altogether. One month later the entire operation was discontinued, the mine abandoned and the property fenced off.

In 1885, the company sold the mine at auction in Vandalia, Illinois, the proceeds all going to cover debts incurred during the brief operation.

Surprisingly, the new owners did not move immediately to reopen the mine. They sent a team of inspectors to evaluate the site and were provided with a report that stated the mine was very rich and could prove extremely profitable if transportation between the remote site and Denver could be improved. It was the last time the new owners had anything to do with the mine.

For the next two decades, mining entrepreneurs traveled to the site of the Entre-Mile Mine and ascertained for themselves that the mine was still very rich and very viable. Several attempts were made to purchase the property, but the owners were never identified. Finally, a Colorado businessman who was intent on buying the

Entre-Mile Mine sent a representative to Vandalia, Illinois, to research the record of the sale. Curiously, though the records were found, the names of the owners remained cryptic and they were never located.

In 1905, an experienced mining engineer went to the Entre-Mile Mine and conducted a thorough evaluation. His report, like the others previously conducted, showed that the mine was still filled with silver, each sample of which assayed out at a high rate of payoff.

The mining engineer found something else, something that would ultimately interfere with the actual extraction of the silver—water had seeped into the 200-foot-deep shaft. Attempts to pump it out proved unsuccessful, for it refilled almost immediately.

In spite of the ownership mystery, several attempts were made by different mining engineers and investors during the next ten years to pump the water from the shaft. Each attempt failed, and eventually the area was abandoned.

Even by today's standards, the location of the Entre-Mile Mine is somewhat remote, and the once-busy roads that led to it have not been used for decades and are sometimes difficult to find. If located, they are even more difficult to negotiate for they are virtually impassible. At the end of those roads, up on the slope of Mount Richtofen, still lies a vast and amazing fortune in silver in the long-abandoned mine. This fortune has tempted many, but the remoteness, along with the difficulty of removing the water to get to the ore, keeps the silver in the earth for now, far from those who desire it so badly.

Black Mountain Gold

The story of the Black Mountain mine is a tale of lost gold that has mystified Colorado residents for almost a century-and-a-half. To this day, it continues to lure gold seekers into the mountains and hills northwest of Fort Collins in search of what is apparently a very rich deposit of ore.

* * *

Sometime during the 1860s, two men, each on foot and leading a burro, arrived in Fort Collins. They came, they said, to purchase some supplies before returning to their mine back at Black Mountain. Black Mountain was located approximately thirty-five straight-line miles to the northwest and in a part of the region not often frequented by prospectors and miners.

During this time, Fort Collins was an active military post, and most of the customers, drinkers, and gamblers seen in and around the small settlement that sprang up around it were uniformed soldiers. In particular, the soldiers were fond of spending their wages at one or more of the several saloons and gambling halls in the town, also called Fort Collins.

The two newcomers were directed to the local mercantile which also served as the town bank. Here they purchased beans, coffee, flour, and a few other goods. For this, they paid in gold nuggets, carefully measured out and counted by the proprietor of the mercantile. The gold, claimed the two strangers, came from their mine. When the proprietor asked if they had any more gold with them, one of the men pulled out a small canvas poke and poured out several dozen more nuggets. The owner purchased these, paying the men $200.

With their new-found wealth, the two men, one an Irishman and the other a German, decided to stop at a nearby tavern and celebrate. Most of the patrons, they noticed, were soldiers. The celebration lasted for two full days and nights, and in the process many of the townsfolk learned about the gold mine somewhere in or near Black Mountain from the inebriated and talkative strangers. Fortunately, the two men did not provide precise directions.

On the third day as the two miners loaded their burros they noticed they were being observed by a few men lurking behind the doors and windows of nearby businesses. When they finally set out on the trail for the return trip to Black Mountain, they noted they were being followed by three of the men they shared drinks with at the tavern. Concerned the trackers, all wearing the uniforms of U.S. Army cavalrymen, were intent on learning the location of their mine, the Irishman and the German led them on a circuitous route through the foothills, doubling back several times, and eventually losing them.

Ten weeks later, the two miners reappeared in Fort Collins, this time leading three burros. The third burro transported two heavy packs containing gold, all of which was purchased by the proprietor of the mercantile.

Following the purchase of supplies and equipment, the two men embarked on another drinking binge at the tavern, this one lasting for three days.

The soldiers who frequented the tavern had been expecting the miners to return, and they were better prepared this time, they thought, to track them back to their diggings. The troopers had pooled some of their money and paid an Indian scout to follow the two men and report back to the Fort on the exact location of the gold mine.

On the morning the two miners left Fort Collins, it was snowing hard and a cold wind was blowing in from the northwest. Suspecting they would be followed again, they purposely took a long and convoluted route, taking several days to make their way back to the mine. During the time they spent on the trail, the snowstorm increased in fury. The Indian tracker was unprepared for the harsh and freezing weather. In addition, he ran out of food, so he turned back.

On their third trip to Fort Collins, the miners went straight to the town's livery, sold one of their burros, and purchased an ox, explaining to the liveryman that the burro was not strong enough to carry all the gold they had mined and accumulated. This comment caught the attention of other customers who were in the livery at the time, and before the day was over this information had spread throughout the town. As was their custom, the two miners indulged in yet another celebration at the tavern, this time buying drinks for all who lasted for the three days of revelry.

Expecting once again to be trailed when they left town, the Irishman and the German were relieved to learn the soldiers had been called away on an assignment. The return trip back to the mine on Black Mountain was uneventful.

When next the two men arrived in Fort Collins, their ox reportedly "stumbled under the weight of the gold it transported." After converting their ore to cash, the miners now found themselves very wealthy men, and treated any and all who wished to celebrate with them to several rounds of drinks at the tavern. This party lasted almost a week before the two returned once again to Black Mountain.

Three months later, the two miners returned to Fort Collins, this time following the spring thaw which had melted most of the snow in the passes. Arriving in town with only two burros, they were asked about their ox. They replied that a bear had killed the ox, so they only brought with them what gold could be transported by the burros. As was now their custom, they retreated to the tavern for drinks after purchasing needed supplies. This celebration, however, would prove to have disastrous consequences.

Approximately ten days into the celebration, the Irishman and the German entered into a protracted argument. It soon grew loud, hostile, and violent, and before anyone could stop him, the Irishman shot and killed the German.

The soldiers who were helping the two men celebrate immediately saw the killing as an opportunity to finally learn the location of the gold mine on Black Mountain. The uniformed troopers told the Irishman if he did not lead them to the mine they would hang him for the murder of his friend. The Irishman flatly refused.

Intending only to frighten him into taking them to the mine, the soldiers located a rope, fashioned a hangman's noose at one end, and placed it around the neck of the drunk Irishman. Leading him out of the tavern and into the livery, they tossed the other end of the rope over a stout beam, and hoisted the Irishman up such that his feet dangled two or three feet above the ground. As the soldiers laughed, the Irishman kicked and flailed at the end of the rope, gagging and his eyes bulging. When they were certain the Irishman knew they were serious about hanging him, they let him fall to the ground. The Irishman tried vainly to rise one or twice, and eventually fell back to the ground and lay still. One of the soldiers, kneeling close to the fallen man, stated he was dead. The soldiers, not wanting to be found at the scene, fled.

When the body of the Irishman was found the next morning by the livery owner, the sheriff was summoned. In spite of an investigation, no one was ever charged with his murder.

With the two miners now dead, several attempts were made to locate their gold mine somewhere in or near Black Mountain, but none were successful. As time passed, the story of the Black Mountain gold mine faded, repeated only now and again by old timers in the region.

Thirty-five years following the death of the Irishman, interest in the Black Mountain gold mine came to the fore once again as a result of a lost boy.

Not far from Fort Collins and located near the Cache La Poudre River was the town of Manhattan. The thriving little community served area miners and lumbermen. Several businesses, including a sawmill, were established and for a time it looked as though Manhattan might rival Fort Collins as the dominant settlement in the region.

One afternoon, the owner of the sawmill reported that his nephew, visiting from somewhere in the east, was missing. He said the youngster, about twelve years old, had mounted a burro and rode off into the mountains to the north and had not returned at the appointed time.

A number of search parties were formed and fanned out into the foothills. They searched for the youngster throughout the night and into the next day but found nary a trace. On the afternoon of the second day as more search parties were being organized, the boy rode into town on the burro. After being taken to his uncle, he told a most amazing story.

The nephew said he was enjoying his ride into the wilderness so much that he lost all track of time and direction. He had given the burro its head and allowed the animal to travel wherever it wished. Presently, the boy decided, he was lost.

The burro he was riding was following a very old and very narrow trail, gradually climbing a low slope leading to Black Mountain. At the end of the trail in a small clearing stood a weathered, dilapidated old cabin made from spruce logs, no doubt cut from the adjacent forest and skidded to this spot.

Dismounting from the burro, the boy explored around the cabin, encountering what he was certain were the bones of a long dead ox. After entering the cabin, he found several pouches stacked on a shelf, each one containing what he thought were gold nuggets. He placed one of the pouches in his pocket.

As the boy related his experiences, he produced the pouch from his pocket. A quick examination of the contents revealed it was, indeed, filled with gold.

William Mellins, a local lumber hauler, was familiar with the story of the Black Mountain gold mine, and on hearing the boy's story was convinced the youngster had found it. When he pressed the youth for details and directions, he was disappointed to learn the boy had no idea where he had been and likely stood little chance of ever finding it again.

Encouraged by the validation that the Black Mountain gold mine did, in fact, exist, and that at the very least there were several more pouches of gold in the far away cabin for the taking, Mellins sold his lumber-hauling rig and made preparations for a trip to Black Mountain. Knowing nothing about mining, rocks, or ore, he hired an old down-and-out prospector who lived in Manhattan, an older man named Pete Parker. Parker lived a hand-to-mouth existence and was often dependent on the charity of others. Several people warned Mellins not to employ Parker, that the old man was not only ignorant about mining but was also crazy and entirely undependable, but so anxious was Mellins to get started on his search for the mine that he ignored their advice.

So it was that the two men, Mellins and Parker, rode out of Manhattan early one morning leading two burros laden with provisions and headed for Black Mountain. For nearly two weeks they searched the foothills of the mountain and the surrounding area but found nothing promising. Eventually, the two men found themselves following a barely discernible trail that wound along the foot of the mountain, gradually climbing to some unknown destination.

After an hour on the trail, the two rounded a bend and were rewarded by the sight of an old weathered cabin set in the middle of a small clearing. Off to the right of the cabin door was a pile of what were clearly ox bones, and in the hillside just beyond the cabin was the opening to a mine shaft.

On spotting the mine, Parker leaped from his burro, screaming, and ran as fast as he could up the path toward the entrance. Mellins, surprised by Parker's sudden burst of energy, dismounted and watched as the old man disappeared into the shaft.

Ten seconds later Parker emerged from the shaft running full speed, and behind him was a large grizzly bear in pursuit. Mellins quickly pulled his rifle from the scabbard tied to his burro, cocked it, and aimed. Unfortunately, the frightened Parker was between him and the bear and Mellins couldn't shoot.

Without lessening his speed, Parker ran headlong into Mellins and tried to seize his rifle. As a result, the two tumbled to the ground as the bear reared up on its hind legs only inches away. Mellins managed to pull the trigger on the rifle, and the subsequent explosion frightened the grizzly sufficiently enough to send it scampering into the trees.

Parker, crazed from the excitement, jumped up and threatened to kill Mellins, and nearly an hour passed before the former lumber hauler managed to calm the old prospector down.

Finally, the two men entered the old cabin, found the remaining sacks of gold nuggets, and placed them in the burro packs. Realizing it would be impossible to remain in the area with the crazy and eccentric Parker, Mellins suggested they return to Manhattan. On the trail to town, Parker, taking his burro, simply walked away toward the southeast, never to be seen again. Years later a skeleton was found several yards off the road to Denver in an abandoned campsite. While it was never proven, many believed it was the remains of Pete Parker.

Over the years, Mellins made three more attempts to find the old cabin and the mine, but got lost each time. Since his unfortunate experience with Parker, Mellins refused to take on another partner during his searches. Mellins himself admitted he was not much of an outdoorsman and had a poor sense of direction, both of which likely contributed to his constantly getting lost in the mountains.

When he was a much older man and long after he had given up searching for the Black Mountain Gold Mine,

Mellins told anyone who would listen that he was convinced the mine was on the north slope of the mountain and closer to the top than to the foothills. He also maintained the cabin was difficult to see from only a few dozen yards away because it was surrounded by a dense coniferous forest. The old narrow trail that led to the mountain, once very difficult to locate, was now all but gone, he said, a victim of erosion, landslides, and vegetation growth.

Over the years, several men have come forth to claim they found the old cabin and the mine, only to become lost during the return trip. Undoubtedly, some of these tales were hoaxes, but a few of them had the ring of truth.

As far as can anyone can tell, the Black Mountain gold mine is still located high up on the mountain deep within the forest. All evidence points to the fact that it is almost impossible to find. Even if the location could be learned, all indications are that it is extremely difficult to reach.

The Black Mountain gold mine is, indeed, lost.

DUTCH OVEN GOLD DUST
CACHE AT GRAND LAKE

Grand Lake, a large natural lake located some sixty miles directly northwest of Denver, has become a popular recreation destination with tourists as well as Colorado residents. Fishing, boating, picnicking, hiking, and myriad other activities greet the visitor in this attractive natural setting.

Grand Lake also attracts a somewhat different kind of traveler these days—the treasure hunter—for somewhere on the north shore of the lake, it is believed, is buried a large cast iron Dutch oven filled with one hundred pounds of gold dust. It has laid in this location for approximately a century and half and has eluded searchers for generations. One person, a very young girl, may have actually found the Dutch oven, but unmindful of the rich contents, simply walked away from it.

* * *

It was the spring of 1854, and six friends who had traveled to California were celebrating their successes in the gold fields and making plans to return to their homes in Virginia. After working hard but living well for a little over three years, the six men had accumulated 100 pounds of gold nuggets and dust and were ready to see their family and friends once again.

The six friends arrived in California via steamer which left from a port on the east coast weeks earlier, sailed clear around the tip of South America, and eventually landed at San Francisco. Deciding to save their money and not book return passage on a boat, the six men planned to load their camping gear onto their horses and make their way back overland, living off the land as much as they could and conserving their savings as much as possible. They packed the dust and nuggets into small canvas sacks which, in turn, were loaded into their saddle packs.

After asking for and receiving travel advice from friends and acquaintances, they set out to cross the Rocky Mountains, taking a somewhat northerly route that would take them through Colorado. After several weeks, they found themselves a few miles east of the small settlement of Steamboat Springs when they were attacked by Indians. Though outnumbered four to one, the miners succeeded in fighting off the attackers as a result of superior firepower. Nevertheless, two of them were killed in the skirmish.

After driving off the Indians and burying their dead companions, the remaining four continued eastward. During the next week, they spotted Indians several times but were never approached. In spite of having no further confrontations, the four men worried constantly about their fate. Furthermore, they were concerned that if they had to run from pursuing Indians, that their overloaded horses would not be up to the task.

By the time they reached Grand Lake, they decided to cache the gold as well some of the heavier equipment they were transporting. Grand Lake is located in Grand County, and is approximately twelve miles long and one mile wide. It is believed the men followed a trail that wound past the northern part of the lake. Somewhere along this trail they stopped to set up camp for the night. The following morning as they were packing to leave, the four men agreed they would place all of the gold dust and nuggets into a large cast-iron Dutch oven and bury it near-by. They selected a location near the lake shore next to a "large gray boulder," excavated a hole deep enough to accommodate the oven, and placed it within. After the lid was set atop the oven, the hole was filled.

Since there were a number of other large boulders close by, they decided they needed to mark the location more effectively. One of the men pulled his hunting knife from its sheath and jabbed it into the trunk of an adjacent spruce tree. The shadow of the knife cast by the early morning sun fell across the side of the boulder.

The ensuing days and weeks of travel were uneventful. After leaving the eastern plains of Colorado, the four men entered Kansas, dreading the long journey ahead of them. The worst part of this leg of their journey was boredom and fatigue. Lulled by the endless flat horizons all around them and tired of sitting in the saddle all day, the four friends were completely unaware of and unprepared for the sudden arrival of a band of Indians. They were roused by the sound of approaching hoofbeats. In the several minutes of fighting that ensued, three of the travelers were killed and the fourth somehow managed to escape with a serious leg wound. As luck would have it, the Indians did not pursue him, remaining content to rifle through the belongings strapped to the horses and to take scalps from the three victims.

Many months later, the surviving member of the party finally made it home to Virginia. The horrors of his journey and the deaths of all of his companions left him a broken man. Many times he contemplated returning to the northern shore of the lake and retrieving the Dutch oven filled with gold, but the nightmares of Indian attacks and hardship would return and deter him from doing so.

As the years passed, he told his children the story of the gold, its burial, and the details of the location. When he passed away several years later, his children, using the directions provided by their late father, organized an expedition into the Colorado Rockies in search of the buried Dutch oven. The party reached Grand Lake without incident and spent several days searching. They encountered what they described as "thousands of boulders" but were unable to locate the spruce tree with a hunting knife sticking out of the trunk. Weeks later they returned to Virginia—empty-handed. They made no further effort to find the gold.

In 1888, a trapper who was camped along the shore of Grand Lake found a knife sticking in a spruce tree several yards from his tent. The knife, he said, was very old and rusted, and the tree had grown around the blade enough to make removal very difficult. He tried to pull the knife from the tree but it remained fast, so he decided to leave it there.

In 1901, a group of picnickers from the nearby town of Grand Lake came to the north shore for a Saturday of recreation. On the way back to town that evening, one of the members of the group, a young man, related that, as he and his fiance were walking hand in hand some distance from the shoreline, they came upon a tall spruce tree with a knife deeply embedded in the trunk. They tried unsuccessfully to remove the knife, but finally gave up and continued on their stroll.

In 1925, a fisherman also told of finding the handle of a knife protruding from the trunk of a spruce tree. Thinking he might retrieve the knife, he started cutting down the large tree with his axe, but found the job exhausting and gave up after a couple dozen strokes.

Today, it is unknown if the spruce tree with the hunting knife in the trunk is still standing. Whether it is or not, it remains quite likely that the Dutch oven treasure still lies buried only inches below the surface near a large gray boulder. Which boulder among the hundreds found along the shore is unknown.

The location of the Dutch oven treasure may have been found, but the finder had no idea what it was at the time. During the mid-1950s, a family was spending a weekend camping on the north shore of Grand Lake. As the parents were preparing lunch early in the afternoon of the second day, one of their three children, a daughter eleven years old, walked into camp carrying an old rusted lid to a Dutch oven. When asked where she found it, she explained that is was just sticking out of the ground near a big rock. As she explained, she pointed to some location northwest of the campsite about forty yards away. Not being aware of the tale of the lost Dutch oven cache, the parents and children did not investigate.

Had they returned to the place where the lid was found protruding from the ground, they would likely have found the gold and would be, by most estimates, almost a half-million dollars wealthier.

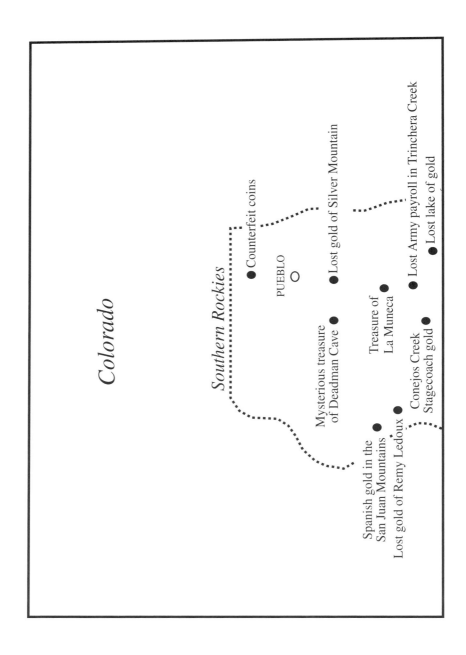

THE SOUTHERN ROCKIES

It was into the southern Rocky Mountains of Colorado that early French and Spanish explorers ventured in search of furs, gold, and silver. And it was these same southern Colorado Rockies that attracted hundreds of miners and prospectors who failed in the gold fields of California and sought new opportunities elsewhere, as well as investors, engineers, and miners who perceived great potential in the abundant ore-bearing rock found here.

The southern Rocky Mountains of Colorado were once a major barrier to travel. High passes—all of them above 9,000 feet and some over 11,000 feet—were difficult to traverse under the best of conditions. When the winter snows filled the passes, they were impossible to cross.

As a result of these geographic and climatic obstacles, most of the emigrant wagon trains going west skirted the southern Colorado Rockies. Furthermore, in the remote and forbidding interiors of the range could be found the homes of warring Indian tribes, most of which posed an additional threat to the travelers.

The principal ranges found in this region include the San Juans, the Sangre de Cristos, the Elk Mountains and the Sawatch. Like the northern Rockies, the southern part is, geologically speaking, millions of years old, and throughout this time was dramatically affected by violent volcanic activity, uplifting, and severe earthquakes, evidence of which can easily be seen today over much of the region.

Centuries ago, French fur trappers encountered outcrops of ore in the southern Colorado Rockies, excavated some, and returned to St. Louis and other points east to relate stories of the incredible wealth that could be found in these remote western environs.

Entire companies of Spanish explorers, miners, engineers, and priests arrived in the Southern Rockies as early as the mid-1600s for a number of reasons: One commonly given was that they were intent on converting what they believed to be heathen savages to Christianity, but while such was going on the Spaniards oriented most of their efforts toward harvesting as much gold and silver from the rocks as possible. It would be difficult to estimate how many hundreds of millions of dollars worth of gold and silver were removed from the southern Colorado Rockies and shipped to Mexico and Spain.

Not all of it, however, arrived at the intended destinations, as the reader shall learn in the tales that follow.

LOST ARMY PAYROLL
AT TRINCHERA CREEK

Trinchera Creek has long been a popular trout fishing
stream located in south-central Colorado. The stream
flows past the town of Fort Garland, and even during the
1880s when this location was a busy army post, it was a
popular fishing spot for the soldiers who were often idle
and had few recreational opportunities.

In 1883, a wooden chest containing an army payroll was
dumped into the creek not far from the fort. The chest, containing an estimated $30,000 in 1880s values, has never
been found.

* * *

In 1852, Fort Massachusetts was constructed not far
from Blanca Peak, some eight miles north of present-day
Fort Garland. This fort was established to house troopers
who, in turn, were assigned to the region to protect settlers, trappers, miners, and travelers from hostile action
by the Ute Indians who deeply resented the white intrusion into their territory. Six years later, it was determined
that this location was less than optimum, and the fort was
moved south near the banks of Trinchera Creek. After the
move, the post was renamed Fort Garland in honor of

Brigadier General John Garland. Initially, the number of troops assigned to Fort Garland was approximately 220. As confrontations with the Utes increased, so did the number of soldiers such that by 1881 at least 1,500 of them were living at the fort.

When not fighting Indians, drilling, or marching, the soldiers stationed at Fort Garland found they had a lot of time on their hands. With little to do, one of their favorite pastimes was to walk down to nearby Trinchera Creek and fish for trout, a welcome diversion from the tedium of everyday military life and an occasional culinary alternative to the usual army dinners served up in the mess hall.

One of the most avid trout fisherman was the paymaster, Lieutenant Leonard Payne. Originally from Ohio, Payne was new to trout fishing, grew to like it very much, and spent every spare moment at his favorite spot downstream from the fort near a wide place in Trinchera Creek.

Sometime in the spring of 1882, Payne was ordered to take a wagon and travel to Fort Union, New Mexico, and pick up the payroll for the Fort Garland troops. Escorted by four armed and mounted guards, Payne set off early one morning on the long journey, several hundred miles to the south.

The trip to Fort Union was relatively uneventful. On arriving, a wooden chest containing the Fort Garland payroll, all in gold coin, was loaded onto the wagon. On the following morning, Payne and his escort set out on the return trip to Colorado.

Other than an occasional traveler, the soldiers saw no one along the way. Concern had been expressed that they might experience problems with wandering bands of Utes, but not a single Indian was seen. Outlaws were becoming more common in New Mexico and Colorado during this time, and though rumors abounded relative to numerous holdups along this route, no such trouble was encountered.

At least, not until they were within sight of Fort Garland.

On the afternoon of the final day of the journey as the wagon rumbled along the road that paralleled a portion of Trinchera Creek, Fort Garland loomed in the distance. On seeing the fort, Payne, grateful the long trip was over, anticipated a few days off duty. He decided he would spend his free time fishing in the stream. Weary from the tedious journey, the escort riders napped in their saddles as the waters of Trinchera Creek gurgled just below.

Suddenly, moments after the party entered Gray Back Gulch, gunshots erupted from the concealment of nearby rocks and Payne and his escort were suddenly startled from their thoughts. At the first volley, three of the troopers fell from their saddles, dead. The fourth soldier, severely wounded, quickly dismounted and took cover behind a nearby deadfall. From this position, he fired his rifle into the ranks of the five oncoming masked riders.

On looking around for the origin of the disturbance, Payne saw several men on horseback riding toward the payroll wagon. Realizing they were outlaws and clearly intent on stealing the gold, the paymaster whipped the horses into a run, hoping to make the gates of Fort Garland before being overtaken. As Payne sped away, he noticed the remaining trooper firing at the outlaws from concealment. Moments later the trooper would be dead, riddled by twelve bullets.

While two of the outlaws reined up to exchange fire with the trooper, the remaining three set off in pursuit of the wagon. During the chase, paymaster Payne was struck in the back by a bullet. In spite of the mortal wound, Payne's efforts were directed toward keeping the payroll from falling into the hands of the outlaws. Letting go of the reins, Payne crawled into the wagon bed and shoved the payroll chest off. After hitting the bank, the chest tumbled end over end down the bank until finally landing in the creek and sinking out of sight in the rushing waters.

By this time, the lookout at Fort Garland spotted the robbery taking place on the road leading to the gate. He sounded the alarm and within minutes, at least one dozen mounted soldiers raced from the fort toward the oncoming runaway wagon. On spotting the troopers, the outlaws turned and fled back down the trail.

Two of the troopers intercepted the wagon, bringing the panicked horses to a halt while the rest of the contingent set off in pursuit of the bandits. In the bed of the wagon, they found Lt. Payne lying in a pool of blood. Initially, they believed the paymaster was dead, but a closer look found him breathing and barely clinging to life. They led the wagon into the fort and summoned the post physician.

After being carried to a cot in the infirmary, Payne grabbed the physician's coat, pulled him close, and told him the payroll chest was in the water at his favorite fishing spot on the creek. Moments later, he lapsed into unconsciousness. By midnight, he was dead. Two days later, Payne and the four escort troopers were buried in the Fort Garland cemetery.

On learning of the fate of the payroll chest, the commanding officer of the post had several of Payne's friends interrogated relative to the location of the late paymasters favorite fishing hole. None of them had any idea where it was, claiming that Payne was somewhat secretive about the select spot and never took anyone fishing with him.

The sloping bank and the adjacent shallow waters of the stream were searched for days by the soldiers, but no sign of the payroll chest was ever found. Some have suggested that the swift waters of Trinchera Creek carried the chest some considerable distance downstream. Others are convinced the wooden chest filled with gold coins was much too heavy to have been influenced by the current, and likely lies close to where it first entered the stream. Regardless, the chest has never been found.

But over a century later, some of the coins were discovered!

In 1975, a fly-fisherman was trying his luck up and down Trinchera Creek near Fort Garland when he made a most amazing discovery. In the shallow waters of the stream near the bank that paralleled a road, he spotted the reflection of something shining on the bottom of the creek. Retrieving the object, he was surprised to discover it was a gold piece, one similar to those associated with army payrolls long ago.

At the time he found the coin, the fisherman had not heard of the story of the lost payroll chest. He simply pocketed the gold piece and showed it to friends and acquaintances from time to time.

Several years after finding the gold piece, the fisherman showed it to an uncle who was familiar with the tale of the missing chest. After relating the story to his nephew, the two men made arrangements to travel to the location to see if they might be able to find the rest of the long lost payroll gold.

On returning to Trinchera Creek, the fisherman had difficulty remembering the exact point at which he found the gold piece. The two men searched up and down the creek for a considerable distance but ultimately came away with nothing.

Another gold piece was discovered ten years later in approximately the same location. The finder pocketed the coin and kept it as a curiosity. As with the discovery in 1975, this fisherman likewise had no knowledge of the lost payroll chest. When the finder returned to the site several weeks afterward, he was delighted with the accidental discovery of six more coins. Yet a third trip to the location, only about a mile from Fort Garland, yielded another three gold pieces.

During the time that has elapsed since the payroll chest tumbled into the rushing waters of Trinchera Creek, the wood has likely rotted away, spilling its golden contents onto the bottom of the stream not far from the bank. At least one researcher has suggested that the chest may have actually broken open on landing at the bottom of the creek. The gold coins, possessed of significant weight, would not be as likely to be washed downstream as would similar sized cobbles. As a result, the vast majority of them remaining in the creek are probably close to where they first landed well over a century ago.

By all accounts, a fortune in gold coins remains in the stream, waiting to be plucked from the cold waters by a lucky fisherman or treasure hunter.

The Lost Gold
of Silver Mountain

During the late 1860s, a prospector and miner named Jack Simpson made three seperate trips to the smelter at Walsenburg. On each trip he led a pack train of seven mules, each heavily loaded with gold-bearing rock. When the ore was removed from the rock matrix, it assayed at approximately $40,000 per ton, an impressive amount for those days. Following each of his trips, Simpson sold his gold for a great deal of cash which he carried back with him to his mine.

Simpson transported the gold to Walsenburg from where he mined it, some "forty to fifty miles to the northwest," he said. Many asked him about the precise location of his gold mine but he remained silent, saying only that it was at Silver Mountain in the Sangre de Cristo range. Silver Mountain was located a few miles northwest of the town of La Veta. While in Walsenburg, Simpson was approached on two occasions by men who expressed an interest in buying him out, but he told them their offers amounted only to a small fraction of what he could dig in just a few days.

As a result of his growing wealth and his secret gold mine, Simpson eventually became a well-known figure around Walsenburg, and before returning to his mine following his third trip, he told several residents that after delivering his next load of gold, he was going to move into town.

It was not to be. Simpson's scalped and mutilated body was discovered on the La Veta-Walsenburg road several days later—he had been attacked and killed by Indians.

On learning of Simpson's death, several men traveled to Silver Mountain to try to find his gold mine but were unsuccessful. The search for the mine continued for several years, and prospectors from as far away as Texas and Pennsylvania arrived in the area to look for it, but its location eluded them. In 1887, a man named Alex Cobsky arrived in Walsenburg. A reclusive sort of man from Ohio, Cobsky spent many days hiking throughout the region, looking, as he told those who asked, for a place to settle. Eventually, he acquired a small herd of goats and moved to a location along the slopes of Silver Mountain. Here, he constructed a simple one-room cabin and lived a simple, uncomplicated life far from the company of other humans. It was the way Alex Cobsky wanted it.

Little was seen of Cobsky during the ensuing years save for the infrequent visits he made to La Veta or Walsenburg in order to purchase supplies. When he did arrive he was always seen wearing several layers of clothes. His hair and beard had grown long and was somewhat unkempt.

One day in February 1901 he arrived in Pueblo, some fifty miles north of Walsenburg, leading a pack train of mules. After asking directions, Cobsky herded the mules to one of the town's smelters and began unloading an immense quantity of gold ore. An assay was performed, and the gold was valued at $40,000 per ton, the same as Simpson's gold over thirty years earlier. Cobsky insisted he be paid in gold coin.

The news of Cobsky's gold spread throughout the region and was even featured in a Denver newspaper. Before long, most of the people familiar with Simpson's find decades earlier were convinced that Cobsky had found the gold mine of the late Jack Simpson.

Two or three times a year for several years, Cobsky transported gold into Pueblo, sold it, and accepted only gold coin as payment. After being paid, Cobsky would remain in town only long enough to consume two or three ice cream sodas before returning to the mountains to the south and west from whence he came. It has been estimated that during the time Cobsky sold his ore to the smelter, he pocketed well over $100,000. Other than ice cream sodas, he was never known to have spent any of the money in Pueblo, and folks assumed he cached it somewhere near his residence on Silver Mountain.

Cobsky was followed from time to time. During his return trips after his first two visits to Pueblo, he took great pains to elude his trackers. Eventually, he gave up and allowed them to follow him all the way to Silver Mountain, but all the trackers ever saw was Cobsky's crude cabin and his equally crude goat pen. Though they searched the mountainside over and over, none could ever discern the location of his gold mine.

As time passed, Cobsky visited Pueblo and La Veta more frequently. Sometimes he arrived without a pack train of gold, remained in town for two or three days drinking ice cream sodas, and then returned to the mountains. Over time, the reclusive Cobsky even grew friendly with some of the La Veta citizens and delighted in the occasional conversations he shared with them.

Cobsky became close with one person in particular, a young boy named Ted Gibbons. Cobsky even invited Gibbons to come and visit him at Silver Mountain, and

Gibbons made several trips to spend time with his new friend.

In 1937, Alex Cobsky, now a wealthy man, led a gold-laden mule train into Walsenburg. After selling his gold he made a few visits and, as was his habit, devoured some ice cream sodas. While leading his empty pack train out of town, Cobsky was struck by a motorcar. The burro he was riding was killed and Cobsky himself suffered a fractured leg, a broken collar bone, and several broken ribs. He was taken to the hospital in Pueblo where it was discovered he suffered additional serious internal injuries.

Cobsky remained hospitalized for over a year, finally passing away as a result of complications. Several people visited Cobsky in his hospital room and tried to persuade him to reveal the location of his gold mine and what many presumed to be a huge cache of gold coins from the sale of his gold in town. He refused to divulge any information whatsoever, and eventually asked the interrogators to leave him alone.

Cobsky passed away one night in his sleep. With his death, most people believed, went the secret to the location of his gold mine.

Not so, for shortly after Cobsky passed away, young Ted Gibbons came forth and stated that he had visited Cobsky's gold mine on several occasions, and then related a most amazing story.

Gibbons told interviewers that Alex Cobsky, in spite of being a recluse, was a rather friendly man who, though very shy and insecure, enjoyed the company of others. At Cobsky's invitation, Gibbons traveled to his residence on Silver Mountain. Only fourteen years old, Gibbons was little interested in or impressed by gold mines, but looked forward to hunting deer and elk with Cobsky along the flanks of the mountain.

After showing Gibbons the location of the gold mine, Cobsky made the boy promise never to reveal the location to anyone. Gibbons agreed, in part because he liked Cobsky, but also because he was convinced if he told anyone about the mine that Cobsky would likely kill him.

Gibbons saw the opening to the mine shaft the moment he entered Cobsky's cabin—the crude log structure was constructed right on top of it! Not only was the mine still producing impressive quantities of very rich ore, it was also where Cobsky cached the proceeds of the sale of the gold.

Few people believed Gibbons story. If true, they said, why did he not return to the mine following Cobsky's death and mine the gold for himself. Gibbons said he wanted to very badly, and was sorely tempted from time to time, but Cobsky, he explained, had trapped the mine such that no one but him could ever enter it without being killed.

A short distance down the shaft from the opening, according to Gibbons, was a very heavy metal door. Beyond that door, Cobsky told Gibbons, was more gold than a man could even dream about, but stated no one would ever be able to retrieve it but him. Inside the shaft and beyond the metal door, Cobsky went on to explain, were carefully concealed metal traps set to snag any intruder. Furthermore, at various places in the mine were a number of dynamite charges rigged to explode if anyone passed without disarming them. As if that weren't bad enough, Cobsky also placed dozens of rattlesnakes in the shaft.

After Cobsky's death, his cabin, never structurally sound to begin with, collapsed. Some years later, according to a Walsenburg newspaper, a severe rockslide obliterated any evidence of Cobsky's old cabin as well as the mine entrance.

Cobsky's closest relatives were two nieces who lived in

Denver. On learning of Cobsky's death they expressed little interest. On being apprised of his apparent great wealth, however, they became very interested and, with the help of others, made several attempts to locate the site of Cobsky's old cabin, and eventually, they hoped, the gold mine. Each attempt ended in failure.

Gibbons was approached and asked to lead a group of men to the site of Cobsky's mine. He agreed to do so for a payment of several thousand dollars. However, on reaching Silver Mountain became lost and disoriented and eventually came away finding nothing.

People living around Walsenburg, La Veta, and Pueblo have taken to referring to the Silver Mountain treasure as the Lost Cobsky Gold Mine. Abundant documentation exists supporting the facts that Cobsky, and Simpson before him, transported large amounts of gold from this region to the smelters in Walsenburg and Pueblo, and subsequent transactions yielded impressive payments in both cash and gold coin.

Verification of the existence of the lost gold mine has never been lacking. The actual location, however, has eluded people for well over a century.

Perhaps a future landslide will uncover the opening to the Lost Cobsky Gold Mine, but finding it will only be part of the problem associated with retrieving the wealth hidden inside. Once the mine is located, the finder must negotiate all of Cobsky's traps.

THE LOST GOLD
OF REMY LEDOUX

During the 1780s, a party of some forty Frenchmen made their way up the Mississippi River to St. Louis and thence across Missouri, the Kansas plains, and into Colorado. The leader of the expedition, one Remy Ledoux, learned of the potential for rich deposits of gold in Colorado's San Juan Mountains from trappers who returned from that remote location to the Crescent City.

With funding from a variety of sources, including Baron de Carondelet, the French governor of Louisiana, Ledoux recruited men for the journey. While he wished for experienced miners and engineers, he was able to hire only men who were living on the streets of New Orleans and looking for work, any kind of work. Nonetheless, Ledoux was impressed with his charges and possessed of good instincts about this trip. He set off for St. Louis and the west with a feeling of buoyancy and optimism.

After following the Osage Trace across Missouri to the Neosho River, Ledoux led the party of forty men to the Arkansas River and followed that stream to the tiny settlement of Pueblo and then on to the Sangre de Cristo Mountains to the west. Game was plentiful along the way and the men looked forward to a year in the wilderness searching for and, hopefully, finding gold. The group found some gold in small quantities in a creek in the Sangre de Cristos, but not enough to keep them there for longer than two weeks.

After crossing the Sangre de Cristo Mountains, the party entered the San Luis Valley, passed through it without incident, and finally arrived near the present-day town of Summitville. After resting men, horses, and mules for a few days, they proceeded into the San Juan Mountains where they found gold in quantities they never dreamed of. After traveling four or five very difficult miles of mountainous terrain southeast of Wolf Creek Pass, they came to a prominence now known as Treasure Mountain. Here, they discovered veins of rich gold in at least three different locations along one side of the mountain. The Frenchmen arrived in late autumn, and already the snows were falling and it was growing bitterly cold.

Despite the severe weather, which worked a hardship on men used to the balmier clime of southern Louisiana, they labored on, digging the rich gold out of the veins and smelting it into eighteen-inch long ingots. As their wealth accumulated and the stack of ingots grew impressively large, Ledoux decided they needed to hide their growing fortune somewhere nearby in the event unwanted visitors arrived. The ingots were carried to and buried in three different sites on the side of the mountain on which the largest and most productive mine was located. Following the caching of the ingots, Ledoux carefully sketched a map on a piece of parchment showing the locations of the caches.

Eventually, the party ran low on provisions. Between the now scanty food supply and the freezing cold, Ledoux decided they should return to the low country until the winter passed in the mountains. Before returning, they would replenish their provisions. The nearest settlement of any consequence was Taos, some 120 miles to the southeast. Before leaving, they covered the openings of the mines to make them look much like the rest of the mountain.

Several days later they arrived in Taos. In order to allay suspicions that they were conducting a mining operation, Ledoux told inquirers they were a surveying party that had been commissioned by the Spanish governor of Louisiana to map the boundary of the former French possession.

The Frenchmen spent the rest of the winter in Taos enjoying the food, drink, and women that were available there. All of their expenses were paid for with cash provided by Carondelet, for Ledoux insisted that all of the gold they extracted from the mine be left at the mountain lest they arouse suspicions among the Taosians.

Eventually, as the weather began warming and the snows retreated, the party made preparations to return to Treasure Mountain and resume the mining of the gold.

On arriving at the site, the Frenchmen eagerly threw themselves into the work of digging the gold. They were refreshed from the restful winter in Taos, and they were also anxious to add to their already sizeable accumulation of ingots, for each was growing eager to return to New Orleans a rich man.

Several weeks later, two of the men collapsed during the work and had to be carried back to their tents. A number of others in the group appeared weak and gaunt and had difficulty wielding their picks and shovels. As the days passed, more and more of the workers collapsed, and several died. After pondering the cause of this dilemma for some time, Ledoux finally decided the men were suffering from scurvy. Their meat-rich and fruit- and vegetable-poor diets were taking a toll on the hard-working laborers. Ledoux made tea from the evergreens that grew on the slopes of the mountain in the hope that it would restore health and vigor to his men. While it had some small positive effect, it came much too late, and by the time the spring season was nearly over, approximately half of the men in the original party were dead. Desperate, Ledoux sent six men to Taos to purchase a supply of food appropriate to maintain the health of the workers. By the time they returned several days later, three more had perished.

Despite the tragedies, work on the mine continued apace, and two more shafts were opened where veins of gold were discovered in exposed rock ledges. The ingots continued to accumulate and the caches, each now containing millions of dollars worth of bullion—some have estimated as much as thirty million dollars—were full.

Shortly after the opening of the two new shafts, the gold vein in the first mine pinched out and was exhausted a short time later. The new mines yielded quantities of gold, but not on the order of the first, and they, too, were soon depleted. By this time, the Ledoux party was down to only twenty men.

Ledoux decided the best course of action would be to return to St. Louis, assemble an additional group of men to serve as an escort, and return to Treasure Mountain to retrieve the gold. Before leaving, Ledoux made a very detailed map of the area, indicating the location of the active mines and the three caches. Then, he had the mines closed down and covered over and the caches likewise camouflaged to appear like any other part of the mountain. This done, the Frenchmen loaded up their pack animals and rode away.

The party headed northeast, crossing several rivers until arriving at the Arkansas River just downstream from Royal Gorge. From here, they followed the river across the eastern plains of Colorado and finally arrived at Bents Fort where they remained a few days to rest. By now, the party numbered only seventeen. Late afternoon of the day they departed the fort, they were approaching the Purgatorie River where they intended to camp for the night when they were attacked by a raiding party of Kiowa Indians. In the skirmish that followed, five of the Frenchmen were killed.

Dispirited and dejected, Ledoux and his party finally made it into western Kansas. Now faced with a long and tedious journey across the seemingly endless semi-arid plains toward the east, they plodded onward.

It wasn't long before they were attacked again by Indians, this time by a party of Pawnees. When the fighting was over, only five Frenchmen were left alive, including Ledoux, who was badly wounded. Whatever money Ledoux had remaining from the original investment from Carondelet was lost during this fight.

Several weeks later—gaunt, weak, and out of provisions—Ledoux, accompanied by only two men, arrived at Kansas City. Here they rested for several weeks trying to regain their strength and preparing themselves to continue on to New Orleans. What happened to the third member of the party can only be conjectured, but when Ledoux boarded a flatboat to follow the Missouri River to St. Louis, he was accompanied by only one man. In St. Louis, Ledoux's remaining companion died. Alone, Remy Ledoux finally returned to New Orleans.

On arriving in the Crescent City, Ledoux asked for and was given an audience with Governor Carondelet, wherein he reported on the long journey westward, the discovery and mining of gold, the huge caches of gold ingots, the disastrous return trip, and the deaths of all of his men.

Carondelet explained to Ledoux that it was not an appropriate time to fund another expedition into the Colorado mountains. For one thing, he said, France was undergoing political turmoil and Napoleon was about to be named Emperor. Men loyal to the French government, such as Carondelet himself, were likely to be deposed, if not assassinated. Besides, Carondelet told Ledoux, his story was too incredible to be believed.

Nothing more was ever heard from Remy Ledoux. It was rumored that, because of no financial support and in poor health, he was unable to return to Treasure Mountain to recover the fortune in gold and eventually died in New Orleans a broken and dispirited man. Others claim he did, in fact, acquire some funding, assembled a large party of men, and traveled west. Somewhere in Texas, according to some researchers, the party was attacked by Comanches and everyone slaughtered. Years passed, and the part of Colorado in which Treasure Mountain was located now belonged to Spain.

In 1842, another party left New Orleans, this one consisting of forty men and headed by the grandson of Remy Ledoux. The young Ledoux, whose first name is variously given as Paul, Carl, and Pierre, led the group on a southerly route through Texas, New Mexico, and eventually into the San Juan Mountains. The grandson had in his possession the original map drawn by Remy Ledoux, the map showing the location of the covered-over gold mines and, more importantly, the three huge caches of gold ingots. Trailing the party was a herd of some sixty mules. Several of the animals were loaded with provisions, but most were intended to transport the gold back to New Orleans.

On arriving in the San Juans, the grandson soon realized that, while his map appeared to be complete and quite detailed relative to Treasure Mountain and the location of the gold caches, it provided no information at all with regard to the exact location of the mountain. The men traveled throughout the range, and the grandson sent out small exploration parties in search of the correct site. Here and there during their travels, they came upon signs left by the Remy Ledoux party, signs consisting principally of a fleur-de-lis scratched into exposed rock. Believing these signs were pointing to the gold caches, the group spent inordinate amounts of time ranging across the area only to finally realize the signs simply marked the trail. In spite of the setbacks, the grandson was convinced they were getting closer to the treasure.

Weeks turned into months, and still no treasure was to be found. Finally, the grandson abandoned the range and returned to New Orleans. The following year, he outfitted another expedition to Colorado, and, once again armed with the map of his grandfather, set out to reclaim the vast fortune he was convinced lay buried somewhere along the slopes of the elusive Treasure Mountain. Unfortunately, while crossing the San Juan River on entering the range, the grandson was thrown from his horse and drowned. The map, as well as other important papers, were said to have been lost in the river.

The grandson's body was recovered by a man named William Yule. After learning the reasons behind the expedition, Yule became interested in searching for Remy Ledoux's lost treasure himself. Receiving a stake from a wealthy rancher in the area, Yule spent the next several years exploring the San Juan Mountains in search of Treasure Mountain and the gold.

During this time, one of the more successful Colorado prospectors was a man named Asa Poor. During his frequent trips into the San Juans and other southern

Colorado ranges, Poor found enough gold to make him well off financially. Poor was casually acquainted with Yule and knew of his quest to find the lost gold of Remy Ledoux. For his part, Poor did not believe in tales of lost gold and buried treasures and considered Yule a bit of a fool for spending so much time and energy looking for something that Poor was convinced did not exist.

Poor changed his mind one evening during a visit with Yule. After dinner and drinks, Yule confessed to possessing the map drawn by Remy Ledoux, the map showing the location of the gold caches. Yule found it, he said, in a leather pouch he recovered when he pulled the grandson's body from the San Juan River. The only problem with the map, he told Poor, was that, while it was very detailed and complete, it provided no information whatsoever on the actual geographic location of Treasure Mountain.

The skeptic Poor, on inspecting the map himself, now became a believer. On the map, he noticed, was marked the location of a grave near the base of Treasure Mountain, the grave of one of Ledoux's men who succumbed to scurvy some sixty years earlier. Poor recalled seeing such a grave at the base of a mountain located in the San Juan range. Committing as much of the map as possible to memory, Asa Poor set out in search of Treasure Mountain.

Eventually, in the spring of 1870 Poor located the grave indicated on Ledoux's map. He dug into it and found the skeleton of a man dead at least half a century. Buried with the skeleton were weapons and tools of European manufacture. Poor knew he was in the right location, but so much time had passed since he had seen the map that he had forgotten most of the directions and landmarks. He decided to try to find Yule and try to purchase the map from him.

After buying the map from Yule, Poor solicited funding

from a prominent miner and the regional Indian agent named Leon Montoy. Montoy was also the superintendent of a productive mine at Summitville and very knowledgeable about the geology of the San Juan Mountains. Poor and Montoy, accompanied by a group of laborers, traveled to the location of the grave. Here, Poor opened the map and read, "Stand on the grave at the foot of the mountain, at six o'clock on a September morning, facing east, and where the shadow of your head falls, you will find the gold."

With some difficulty, Poor and Montoy found one of the mines worked by Ledoux and his Frenchmen. Though they searched and searched for the three caches of ingots, they met only with failure. As Montoy was to later write, "years of avalanches and rockslides caused tons of rubble to be deposited atop the likely locations of the gold caches."

The buried gold of Remy Ledoux remains hidden near the base of Treasure Mountain, hidden for well over two centuries. Though occasional searches for this fantastic treasure are still undertaken, it has never been found. It lies beneath the rock and debris of the mountain, still luring adventurers and treasure seekers from all over the world.

SPANISH GOLD IN THE SAN JUAN MOUNTAINS

Somewhere in the northeastern part of Colorado's Archuleta County where the San Juan Mountains rise in prominence lies what many researchers contend may be one of the most incredible caches of gold ore and bullion on the North American continent. The gold—some estimates run as high as one hundred million dollars worth in today's values—is buried in an old Spanish mine shaft, the very shaft from which the gold was excavated.

This amazing treasure has attracted the attention of searchers and researchers for generations, but most are convinced it still lies deep below the surface, still tempting those who come from the four corners of the world to look for it.

* * *

Sometime during the 1580s, the Spanish soldier/explorer Juan de Onate organized the settlement of a small community for his followers not far from the present-day town of Chama, New Mexico. Using this as his base of operations, Onate sent parties of surveyors, miners, and soldiers into the San Juan Mountains lying to the north in what is now Colorado. Their orders were to find gold and silver, mine it, smelt it, and ship it to the treasuries of mother-land Spain to finance even more explorations in the New World as well as ongoing war efforts in Europe.

Gold was indeed found in the San Juans, and plenty of it, but the Spaniards were too few to defend themselves adequately against the constant Indian attacks. As time passed and more and more of the Spaniards fell to the arrows and spears of the Indians, it became prudent to abandon the San Juans and return with a larger force some time in the future. That time never came, however, and soon afterward Spanish dominance in this region weakened and eventually ceased altogether.

One of the Spaniards assigned to the mines in the San Juan Mountains kept very detailed and meticulous jour-nals of the excavation and smelting operations as well as accounts of daily life among the miners in this remote region. Included in the journals was a precise inventory of the gold extracted, smelted, and readied to be shipped back to Spain.

The journals, along with other items from the expedi-tion, eventually wound up being stored in a monastery in Spain where they remained untouched until 1765. At that time, a French scholar who was studying in the monastery found them, read them over and over, and eventually became enthralled at the possibility of so much gold lying in the mountains in a place he had never heard of across the sea. Eventually, he determined he would go search for the location and mine the gold himself.

For the next five years, the Frenchman traveled the European countryside soliciting financiers to invest in his idea. He was remarkably successful, and in 1770, he, along with a party of over 300 men, including laborers, miners, engineers, geologists, surveyors, and armed guards, sailed from the French port of Le Havre, crossed the Atlantic, and arrived in New Orleans some three months later. Here, they purchased supplies and equipment, along with approximately 600 horses and mules. Thus equipped, the gold-seeking party set out overland to the San Juan Mountains.

Following the directions provided in the old journals, the Frenchmen arrived in the San Juans at the precise location where the Spaniards mined the gold. Almost immediately, the newcomers reopened the old shafts, began excavating new ones, and in a very short time were accumulating a sizeable quantity of gold ore. In all, nine shafts were being worked, and all of them were yielding impressive amounts of gold. Working around the clock, the laborers extended the shafts deep into the mountains, and it was estimated that several miles of tunnels were dug. As the ore was taken from the mines, it was separated from the quartz matrix in one of the several arrastres set up nearby and then smelted into ingots. Before much time had passed, hundreds, perhaps thousands, of gold ingots began piling up at several locations around the mining camp.

Throughout the period of time the French miners occupied this area, they were subjected to numerous Indian attacks. At first the attacks occurred with stunning frequency, most likely because the Indians resented the intrusion of the newcomers into their homelands. For a time it was difficult for the Frenchmen to venture out of the camp to hunt meat or gather firewood because they would invariably be set upon by the Indians. In time, however, the attacks lessened, but the French leader kept guards posted around the camp just to be safe.

The leader of the expedition subsequently established a headquarters some distance away and at a location that was eventually to become the present-day town of

Summitville. To this location the gold ingots were delivered, counted, and stored until such time as they were to be shipped back to New Orleans.

For nearly five years the Frenchmen labored in the mines. Since each of them was working for a share, they went about their daily labor with enthusiasm, knowing that they would all return to France as wealthy men. As they worked they talked about what they would purchase with their share of the gold. Unfortunately, just as the leader of the party began making plans for the return trip, disaster befell the group.

While the Frenchmen worked in the shafts, mining was also taking place in the adjacent mountains. Newly arrived Spaniards were, like the Frenchmen, seeking their fortunes by digging the abundant gold from the veins found in the San Juans. For almost a year, the Frenchmen were aware of the proximity of the Spaniards, but both groups kept to themselves. The Spaniards regarded the San Juans as Spanish territory and resented the presence of the French, but they were so busy with their own mining activities that they had little time to confront miners on a distant mountain.

That would soon change. After working in the deep mines for several weeks in a row, the Frenchmen were allowed to take some time off. During this leisure time, many of them would travel to Taos or Santa Fe to the southeast and spend their allotment on wine and women. Over time, too many of the French miners spoke too often to the young Spanish women they courted about the fantastic wealth in gold they were digging from the mountainside in the San Juans. The women quickly informed the Spanish miners and soldiers, many of whom frequented Taos and Santa Fe as well. Eventually, this information reached the Spanish officers in Taos. With little delay, preparations were made to attack the Frenchmen and either run them off the mountain or kill them.

Unlike the French, the Spaniards were friendly with most of the local Indians. The Spanish leaders sent emissaries to the various tribes in the locale who convinced the Indians that the Frenchmen were a menace that needed to be eliminated. The Spaniards promised the Indians a hefty bounty for every French scalp brought in.

Within days, Indian attacks on the French mining camp increased in frequency and intensity, and several Frenchmen were killed. The attacks became so regular and successful that after three months the contingent of Frenchmen numbered only slightly less than one hundred. Since they were unable to leave the guarded camp to hunt, provisions ran low and the situation was growing tenuous.

Realizing they could not hope to remain in the area for much longer, the leader decided it would be prudent to seal off the mines and depart, returning only when he could organize a larger force of armed men to repel the attacks of the Indians. Since they were fleeing an aggressive and persistent force, the Frenchmen also determined it would not be prudent to try to transport any of the gold from the area. Instead, the accumulated gold, both ore and bullion, was loaded onto mules and carried to the shaft nearest the Summitville headquarters.

The opening to this shaft was a straight vertical drop of some thirty or forty feet down into which the miners were lowered by rope. At the bottom, the shaft leveled off and ran another fifty feet before terminating. The horizontal part of this shaft was braced with extra timbers. Following this, the ingots were lowered in baskets, carried deep into the horizontal shaft, and stacked against the walls. This done, the leader ordered the vertical shaft filled with rock and dirt. Nearby, several French locator marks were chiseled onto exposed rock faces and slashed onto the trunks of trees. In all, caching and covering the enormous amount of gold took well over a week.

During the hiding of the gold, Indian attacks increased and several dozen more men were killed. Now dramatically low on provisions and manpower, the thirty survivors fled from the area with hopes of reaching New Orleans alive.

Ultimately only a handful made it back. So great were the hardships faced in the mountains and during the long journey to New Orleans that half of the survivors refused to return. The remaining Frenchmen, including the leader, strove for several months to obtain financial backing for a return trip to the San Juans but their efforts were met with rejection. Eventually, all returned to France.

The gold, all 100 million dollars worth of it, remained hidden in the lost shaft somewhere in the San Juans, never to be reclaimed by the Frenchmen or anyone else.

It lies there today.

THE MYSTERIOUS TREASURE OF DEADMAN CAVE

The Sangre de Cristo Mountains are a northwest-southeast trending component of the Rocky Mountains located in southern Colorado. Here and there throughout this range can be found caves, some large, some very small. Many of these caves serve as shelter for the numerous animals that live in the range. Many others, according to the evidence, once served as temporary habitats for early Indians.

There is one cave in the Sangre de Cristo Range, however, that is much, much more. Deep inside this cave lies an unbelievably large cache of gold ingots, all bearing marks of a Spanish smelter. How this gold, millions of dollars worth of it, came to be stored in this cave is a mystery that has never been solved.

* * *

One winter not too many years ago, three Colorado residents were backpacking in the Sangre de Cristo Mountains when they made an unforgettable discovery. The three men—S. J. Harkman, H. A. Melton, and E. R. Oliver—were amateur geologists and avid prospectors from Silver Cliff, Colorado, located several miles to the north. They came to the Sangre de Cristos from time to time to try their luck at panning placer gold in the many streams found here. Though they often found enough of the metal to offset the costs of their expeditions, they remained hopeful of and constantly on the lookout for a promising seam of gold-filled quartz among the exposed rock. Quietly, they talked among themselves of someday making a big strike.

On this particular excursion into the range, Harkman, Melton, and Oliver found themselves deep in the mountains and within sight of Blanca Peak when they were surprised by the appearance of a sudden and unexpected snowstorm. Rather than try to hike out in the blizzard, they decided to seek shelter and await the passage of the storm. Higher up in the narrow, remote canyon in which they found themselves, they spotted a protruding ledge of rock that afforded some protection and made their way toward it. Once safely under the ledge, they found dry wood which they used to make a small fire.

As the three men watched the storm raging just beyond their sanctuary, Harkman, peering through the falling snow, noticed what appeared to be a low, narrow opening to a cave on the far canyon wall just opposite from where they huddled around the fire. About an hour later, and growing bored with sitting around the fire, Harkman suggested they crawl out from under the ledge, cross the canyon floor, and go investigate the cave on the opposite side. After climbing the slope leading to the opening, the three men peered inside.

Oliver, flashlight in hand, crawled into the opening. After he had proceeded several dozen feet, he called back to his companions, telling them that it opened into a chamber big enough to stand in. Moments later, he was joined by Harkman and Melton. After exploring the chamber for several minutes, Oliver found another passageway at the far end.

Single file, the three friends crawled through the passageway for less than a minute when it opened into an even larger chamber. So large was this chamber that, shining their flashlights from the center, the men could barely see the adjacent walls. Very slowly and deliberately, they began exploring around the room.

Moments later, Melton cried out when his foot struck an object in the dust. On closer examination, he saw that it was a human skull! He called to his companions and together the three leaned in for a closer look. Convinced this cave may offer the potential for a significant adventure, the three friends decided to return to the canyon outside and fetch armloads of wood into the cave. The light cast by a large fire, they determined, would aid their exploration of the cave considerably.

When the fire was finally burning well, it lit up the chamber significantly more than did their flashlights. During the course of their subsequent examination of the chamber, the three men found five complete human skeletons and yet another passageway.

Carrying makeshift torches, the three prospectors cautiously entered this new passageway, wondering all the while what they might find next. Unlike the other passages, this one was very rocky and difficult to negotiate. Time and again, the three were forced to climb over or crawl around large rocks. Finally, after traveling about thirty yards, the tunnel opened into another chamber, this one considerably smaller than the first.

As the three rested on the floor of the new chamber, they held their torches high as they examined the room. Against the far wall they discerned a large pile of what they believed to be rocks. Oliver crawled over to the pile and picked up one of the objects. At first, he was surprised by its unusually heavy weight, then, on looking closer he was stunned to see it was a gold ingot! He called to his companions.

After being joined by Harkman and Melton, Oliver held his torch over the pile of objects. After brushing away a heavy layer of dust that suggested the objects had lain in this location for centuries, they discovered that the entire stack consisted of gold bars. They counted 400 of them. On examining several of the bars closely, Melton noticed that each was imprinted with a Christian cross topped with an inverted carat.

An hour later as the three companions discussed their amazing discovery, Harkman noticed two more passage-ways leading from the chamber. They had been so enthralled with the discovery that they had not noticed them until then. Oliver suggested more gold bars might lie beyond, but Melton pointed out that their torches were burning low and their flashlight batteries were almost exhausted. They decided to leave the cavern and make plans for a return trip to recover the gold. Each man car-ried a gold ingot out with him.

By the time they crawled out of the opening to the cave, the storm had abated somewhat, and the three men hiked out of the canyon and to their vehicle. Later that evening, they finally returned to Silver Cliff. Within the week, they had the gold bars assayed and learned that each was worth $900. They also learned that the symbol imprinted on the gold bars identified them as being of Spanish ori-gin, and they assumed that Spaniards had placed the bars in the cave. The last known mining of gold by the Spanish in this region, they subsequently learned, took place approximately four hundred years earlier!

Harkman, Melton, and Oliver each sold their gold bars

and used some of the proceeds to prepare for a return trip to the Sangre de Cristo Mountains to retrieve the remainder of the gold. During their preparations, they spoke often about what they were going to do with their newfound wealth and how they would live the rest of their lives in splendor. During their discussions, the three friends began referring to the remote cave containing the skeletons as Deadman Cave.

Since the winter storm season had set in, they decided to delay their return until sometime in the spring. Despite the lure of great wealth in the remote canyon, they cared little about braving blizzards and negotiating the rocky, rugged, and oftentimes dangerous trails in the icy cold. Waiting for the spring thaw merely heightened their anticipation.

By the time April arrived, the snows in the Sangre de Cristos had melted sufficiently to allow for a return to Deadman Cave. After parking their vehicle in the same place they did on the previous trip, the three hoisted their backpacks and set out to look for the canyon where the cave was located.

As they climbed into the higher reaches of the range and were faced with trails forking off in different directions, Harkman, Melton, and Oliver began to disagree over which was the correct one. They became disoriented several times, and then finally admitted to being lost. As the sun set below the tall peaks and they made preparations for evening camp, the three discouraged treasure hunters were beginning to wonder if they would ever see the four hundred gold ingots again.

For nearly a week, the three men searched for the remote canyon that held the opening to Deadman Cave as well as the protruding ledge under which they took shelter from the snowstorm of the previous season. Ultimately, they found nothing that remotely resembled the canyon, the cave, or the ledge. Discouraged and dejected, they finally gave up and returned home where they immediately started making plans for a return trip.

During the next several successive weekends, the three men returned to the portion of the Sangre de Cristo Mountains they were certain held the location of Deadman Cave, but each trip was met with failure. Finally, after two years of searching, they gave up.

Based on the story related by Harkman, Melton, and Oliver, others have explored throughout the Sangre de Cristo Mountains attempting to find Deadman Cave, but they have been no more successful than those that went before them. Some have suggested that the three men fabricated the entire story, but investigations have proven them honest and credible. Furthermore, several people did, in fact, view the three Spanish-marked gold ingots taken from the cave.

As far as anyone knows, the gold ingots still lie stacked against the wall of the distant chamber of the cavern, still guarded by the skeletons of men long dead. Whoever eventually locates Deadman Cave and finds the gold bars will come into possession of a fortune few have experienced in modern times.

LOST CONEJOS CREEK STAGECOACH GOLD

During the second week of August, 1881, a lone gunman held up a stagecoach near the town of Conejos in southern Colorado near the New Mexico border. Shortly after he escaped with the large gold shipment, his trail was quickly picked up by the local sheriff. Since the weight of so much gold was slowing him down, the robber buried it in two separate locations along the bank of the Conejos River. One of the caches has been found, but the other remains lost.

* * *

During the summer of 1881, a black man named James Thomas arrived in the town of Conejos. Thomas, who lived in a shabby tent on the outskirts of town, walked up and down the dirt streets of Conejos for several days asking questions about stagecoach schedules. He soon learned that an incoming stage from Trinidad in neighboring Las Animas County was transporting several thousand dollars worth of gold coins and ingots. Alerted to Thomas' queries, the local sheriff, D. C. Ogsbury, had him watched by a deputy. Since Thomas broke no laws while he was in town, he was never approached by the sheriff, but he was observed closely nonetheless.

One day before the stage from Trinidad was to arrive, Thomas disappeared. When the sheriff rode out to check his camp, all he found were the cold ashes from the camp-fire and a few empty tins of canned goods. Thomas and the horse he rode were gone.

Later that afternoon, it was confirmed to the sheriff by the stagecoach company that the Trinidad coach was transporting a shipment of gold and would arrive the following day. Recalling Thomas' earlier questions about coach schedules, Sheriff Ogsbury decided he would ride out to meet it.

The next morning, Sheriff Ogsbury finished up his early rounds, mounted up, and rode down the trail to meet the coach. At the same time, approximately one hour's ride up the trail, the coach was halted by a masked gunman leading a spare horse. The driver and the guard, surprised at the presence of the black outlaw, were ordered to throw their weapons to the ground. Following this, they were told to open the chest and toss the gold ingots to the ground. The ingots were taken from a chest and thrown down. The gold coins, packed in several canvas sacks, were likewise thrown to the ground.

After ordering the driver to continue on down the trail toward Conejos, the robber dismounted and loaded the heavy sacks onto his own mount and into packs strapped to the second horse. This done, he rode away.

A short time later, the sheriff met the stagecoach and was informed of the robbery by the excited driver and guard, and the description of the robber convinced Ogsbury that it was Thomas. Knowing he was less than an hour behind the robber, the sheriff set out in pursuit.

After the first two or three miles of riding, Thomas noticed his horses were growing fatigued. The outlaw immediately deduced the added weight of the gold was slowing them down, so he decided to cache some of it and return for it another time.

His escape route paralleled the Conejos River east of town. Presently, he pulled next to the bank of the river, unloaded approximately half of the gold, scooped out a shallow hole in the river bank, and buried it. After riding another two miles, he realized it would be necessary to cache the remainder of the gold. Once again, he reined up at the bank of the river, buried the gold, and continued on. For the moment, Thomas was determined to escape the pursuit he knew would follow once the robbery was reported. He would return for the gold when he was certain lawmen were not looking for him. Little did he know that Sheriff Ogsbury was only minutes behind him.

Shortly after Thomas cached the last of the gold, the sheriff caught sight of him and spurred his horse onward, gradually closing the distance. Thomas' horse, exhausted from transporting the heavy load of gold, was incapable of outdistancing the sheriff, and within the hour, Thomas was captured, cuffed, and led back to Conejos.

After being placed in the Conejos jail, Thomas made arrangements to send a message to his brother, another small-time outlaw known as The Black Kid. The Black Kid, along with three companions, arrived in town about ten days later. It is unclear what The Black Kid's intentions were relative to his brother, but when he and his small gang arrived in town, they went immediately to a saloon and began drinking. Fueled by alcohol, they soon grew belligerent, began threatening some of the customers, and started shooting their revolvers in the saloon. Eventually, the owner summoned Ogsbury.

When Sheriff Ogsbury arrived and tried to calm the four men, he was shot and killed. Deputies arrived a short time later, arrested the malefactors, and placed them in the jail with Thomas. The next night, however, a party of vigilantes broke into the unguarded jail, removed The

Black Kid from his cell, and hung him from the ceiling of a small building adjacent to the courthouse.

Weeks later, James Thomas was convicted of robbing the stage and sent to prison. After serving almost two decades, he was released. According to existing records, Thomas returned to his home in Georgia, and it is almost certain he never returned to southern Colorado to retrieve the buried gold coins and ingots.

* * *

In 1910, two men riding along the bank of the Conejos River were greeted by a remarkable sight. Several days earlier, the river had flooded. At one location not far from the town of Conejos, the swiftly flowing water eroded into an adjacent cutbank and exposed a large amount of gold coins and ingots, causing them to spill down the bank and into the river. The two riders scooped up all of the gold they could find and carried it into town where it was identified as a portion of the loot stolen by James Thomas nearly thirty years earlier.

The discovery of the gold generated a number searches for the remaining loot. For several years, people looking for the treasure ranged up and down the Conejos River digging hundreds of holes in the bank in the hope of locating the buried gold. None were successful.

The gold still lies there today. Perhaps another flood will uncover this remaining cache just as it did the other.

THE TREASURE
OF LA MUNECA

The magnificent Spanish Peaks are located just west of Walsenburg, their spires rising in excess of 13,000 feet. The Spanish Peaks area is primarily of volcanic origin, and remains today an excellent outdoor geology laboratory for college and university students who wish to study associated landforms and processes up close.

Underground masses of granite shaped from the cooled magma are where gold and silver is formed. Occasionally, and long after cooling, such masses are uplifted and exposed by a variety of tectonic forces, and it is to such environments that gold seekers travel in hopes of finding a promising outcrop or ledge from which they can extract the ore and, hopefully, grow wealthy.

Into this very region came a group of Spaniards sometime during the early 1800s. Unlike numerous previous Spanish forays into this region sponsored by the government, this one was privately funded and consisted of a party of only ten or twelve men, all determined to find gold among the igneous intrusive exposures.

Much to their supreme delight, the Spaniards did find gold and plenty of it. So rich were their discoveries that on at least two occasions they sent an impressive amount home to Spain with a promise of more to come.

As with previous and subsequent parties of prospectors and miners who came into this area, the Spaniards were occasionally harassed by the Ute Indians who lived in the region, an indigenous tribe that deeply resented the intrusion of whites into their homelands. Perceiving the Utes as a serious threat, the Spaniards allied themselves with a tribe of their long-time enemies, the Arapahos. With the additional men in camp, the Utes were less inclined to attack. So well did the Spaniards and the Arapahos get along that the Indians were actually given jobs working in the mines. With this extra help, excavations increased and additional shafts were opened up, yielding even more gold.

The chief of the Arapahos had a beautiful daughter whocaught the eye of the leader of the Spaniards, a man named Carlos Montenegro. Montenegro politely requested permission to court the young girl and it was eventually given. In time, the two fell in love and were wed, and before a year passed she gave birth to a daughter.

The mining of gold proceeded for three more years without incident, but soon the area in and around the Spanish Peaks was swarming with other miners. Word of the rich gold strikes traveled as far away as Europe, and before long, hundreds of newcomers came to the area to try their luck. Some found gold, many did not, but all succeeded in rousing the ire of the Utes.

Growing ever more irritated at the rising tide of whites coming into the Spanish Peaks region, the Utes sent word to other branches of the tribe scattered to the north and west to provide reinforcements. Within a few weeks, the number of Utes grew such that they felt confident to launch new and more vigorous attacks on the miners.

Within a short time, the attacks increased in number and intensity and many of the whites were left dead.

Because of the growing presence of hostile Utes, it became more difficult to leave the mining camps to hunt for game. As provisions ran low, it created a hardship on the miners and soon many were starving.

The Arapaho chief sought a meeting with Montenegro and recommended he assemble his followers and leave the area before it was too late, that the Utes were now too many and too powerful to resist. If they did not leave, he said, the miners would likely be killed.

The Spaniards agreed among themselves that they would pack up and leave the area. As they loaded their accumulated hoard of gold ingots into packs and strapped them onto the mules, a Ute war party appeared in the distance riding hard toward the miners. Montenegro told his wife to take their child and remain with her father until such time as he could return for them. Tearfully, she agreed and quietly left with the tribe.

Realizing that the great load of gold would only inhibit their flight, Montenegro ordered it taken to a large nearby rock. The miners scooped out a hole next to it, and deposited their wealth within. The rock, which was approximately thirty feet high, was shaped somewhat like a doll, and the Spaniards had thus named it La Muneca.

After covering the hole containing all of the wealth they had accumulated during the previous years, Montenegro placed a large rock over it, one with a deep, narrow V-shaped groove in the center. Into this cut, he placed one of the metal shovels which was used to excavate the hole. Following this, the Spaniards mounted their horses and prepared to ride hard to escape the warring Indians, but it was too late. No sooner had they pointed their horses toward the trail that would take them from the range than they found themselves surrounded by the Utes. A brief but violent battle ensued, and within minutes the entire party of Spaniards was killed, all but Montenegro and one other, both of whom feigned death and crawled away to hide among some rocks.

From concealment, the two frightened men watched as the Utes scalped and mutilated the bodies of their dead companions. At sundown when the Indians had finished with their bloody work and had stripped any desired clothing and footwear from the corpses, they mounted up and rode away.

When they were certain the Indians had departed, the two Spaniards cautiously made their way through the rocks and trees out of the Spanish Peaks range and walked all the way to Santa Fe, arriving bruised, blistered, tired, hungry, and sore several weeks later. After resting for nearly three months, the two men traveled to New Orleans, boarded a ship and returned to Spain.

Though relieved to be back in his homeland and far from the threat of the Indians, Montenegro missed his wife and daughter terribly and promised himself he would return to them as soon as possible. Time passed swiftly, and it was ten years before Montenegro was able to solicit enough money to finance a trip back to Colorado.

Eventually, he arrived back at the Spanish Peaks and sought the Arapaho village where he knew he would be reunited with his family. After several days of searching he finally located the village only to learn that his wife had died years earlier from a fever. His daughter, however, was thirteen years old and very beautiful, and the two spent many happy days together getting reacquainted.

The loss of his wife proved to be too much for Montenegro to bear, and he finally decided he would go back to Spain without searching for the buried treasure of La Muneca. He begged his daughter to accompany him, but she politely refused, preferring to remain in the country of her people rather than be transported to some place far away and completely unknown to her. Following a tearful goodbye, Montenegro returned to Spain never to see the Spanish Peaks again. Before leaving, however, he told his daughter about the mining of the ore, the attack by the Ute Indians, and the burying of the gold in the shadow of La Muneca. He told her that covering the place where the gold was buried was a rock that held a metal shovel in a narrow crack. He told the young girl how hard he and his companions worked for many years to dig the gold from the mines only to lose it during their flight from the Utes. He told her he came to believe the gold was cursed and that it was meant to remain hidden in the ground for all time.

Five years later, Montenegro's daughter was wed to an Arapaho warrior, a brave man known for his fighting prowess but also for his honesty and integrity. Together they raised two sons.

By the time the sons were in their twenties, the father passed away and the mother, though alive, was in very poor health and she feared she would not live much longer. One day she called her sons to her bedside and told them the story of the lost gold of La Muneca that had been hidden many years earlier. She went to great lengths to tell of the hardships faced by her father while digging the gold in the range of the Spanish Peaks, of the constant Indian attacks, of the final massacre, of the burying of the tremendous amount of gold beneath La Muneca, and the marking of the spot with the curious rock and the metal shovel. She also told them her father believed the gold was cursed and that any who retrieved it would have to endure a lifetime of bad luck.

Two years later the mother passed away and the sons decided they would try to find the gold of their grandfather. With little difficulty, they located the rock known as La Muneca. By this time, La Muneca was a prominent landmark in the region and well known to many.

Though they searched for several days, however, they were unable to locate the rock with the V-shaped niche that contained the metal shovel. Surrounding La Muneca in all directions were hundreds, perhaps thousands, of rocks of all shapes and sizes.

While the brothers were searching for the gold of La Muneca, they set up a camp not far from the noted landmark. Each morning they left camp after breakfast, searched all day, and returned at night. One evening while they were finishing their dinner, they were visited by a rancher who lived not far away. He was out looking for stray livestock, noticed the campfire, and stopped by to investigate.

Without revealing their intentions, the brothers asked the man if he was aware of a rock with a V-shaped niche which contained a metal shovel. Surprisingly, the new-comer told them he found an old and very weathered shovel lying in a large rock the previous year. He retrieved it, fashioned a new handle for it, and used it to clear snow from the front stoop of his house.

Stunned, the brothers asked him if he could relocate the rock where he found the shovel. The man told them no, he could not, for there were thousands of such rocks in the area and he had no recollection of which one yielded the shovel.

Discouraged by this news, the brothers struck camp the following morning and returned to their homes, never again to search for the lost gold of La Muneca.

There exists no compelling evidence to suggest anyone has ever located the place where the large hoard of

Spanish gold was buried. It is a tale known mostly to those who collect and study the stories of lost mines and buried treasures, but not one known to most people. Somewhere in the shadow of La Muneca today lies an odd-shaped stone, one with a V-shaped niche in it that once contained a metal shovel. Beneath that rock, probably only a few inches below the surface, lies untold millions of dollars worth of Spanish gold.

LOST COUNTERFEIT
COINS NOW WORTH $$$

In 1900, hundreds of counterfeit silver coins were produced in Victor, Colorado. The coins were stamped out, not by outlaws, but by a prominent and upright businessman and were intended to be used in legitimate business transactions. These counterfeit coins, though quite illegal, were gratefully accepted by the citizens and the business community of Victor as legal tender and were intended to temporarily offset the growing shortage of U.S. coins in this region. Because of the paucity of money of any kind in many of the somewhat remote mining towns that existed in the area, many of these counterfeit coins were hoarded. Today, some of them bring upwards of $6,000 apiece as collector's items.

* * *

Victor, Colorado, located some twelve miles southwest of Pikes Peak in the central part of the state, was a booming city in 1891. Gold and silver had been discovered throughout much of the area, and soon miners, laborers, businessmen, ministers, ladies of the night, and opportunists flocked to the region, all trying to gather a portion of the new-found wealth. It seemed as though the precious ore that lured them there was encountered with every turn of the shovel and every dip of a gold pan into a promising stream. As a result, the town of Victor, named after the nearby Victor Mine, grew rapidly and was soon filled with businesses, churches, saloons, and other cultural necessities.

A great deal of the gold and silver that was mined from this area was shipped back East to the United States mint at Philadelphia. The process of mining the ore, extracting it, smelting it, and shipping it eastward was a long and tedious one, and a demand soon grew for the establishment of a federal mint in Colorado. Until such time as that could transpire, however, the gold entrepreneurs were forced to deal with this logistical obstacle, often waiting for weeks, even months, for minted coins to be shipped to the region.

One of the consequences of the long process was that many Colorado citizens and businessmen found coins scarce, and, as a result, numerous business transactions had to be postponed or cancelled altogether. Before long, the shortage of gold and silver coins in the region became a serious impediment to conducting business, and quite often transactions involved the somewhat cumbersome process of exchanging gold dust and gold nuggets for goods and services.

These problems were accentuated when other mining towns like nearby Cripple Creek sprang up, and the demand for coins was dramatically increased.

Before long, several railroad companies were laying tracks in the region, dozens of banking and financing operations were springing up, and the towns continued to fill with miners, prospectors, laborers, businessmen, ministers, and others, all of whom placed even heavier demands on the need for coins for transactions.

In 1900, a prominent Victor businessman named Joseph Lesher undertook to solve this problem. A good citizen and a contributing member of the community, Lesher, using a very high grade of silver, began to privately produce coins. The coins were octagonal and one side contained an image of Pikes Peak. They were called the Lesher Referendum Dollars and were used primarily to conduct trade in Victor and a few neighboring towns. The coins were numbered, the names of the businesses that purchased them were stamped onto one side, and they were employed in daily transactions much as any other coin might be. Five different types of coins were minted between 1900 and 1901, each having a different value.

A number of Victor merchants refused to use the Lesher coins, fearing they would be breaking some federal law or another. Others, like businessman Zach Hutton, did not quite understand the purpose and the intended temporary nature of the coins. Hutton believed the Lesher dollars were actually produced by the United States government and he perceived them as real money. Well aware that there was a shortage of coins in the region, Hutton, who had a reputation as a bit of a miser anyway, began hoarding the Lesher dollars as he acquired them, believing that if the shortage continued they would be worth a lot of money in the near future.

As Hutton acquired more and more of the Lesher dollars, he kept them in two large coffee cans. By the end of 1901, Hutton had completely filled the cans with the dollars. Concerned someone might want to steal his collection of Lesher dollars, estimated to be several hundred by now, Hutton hid them someplace on his property.

In January of 1902, Hutton fell ill with a severe case of pneumonia. He was treated for several weeks but finally died. Not long after his funeral, Hutton's house was broken into and thoroughly searched. The perpetrators were apparently thieves looking for his collection of Lesher dollars, but according to reports, they never found them. Around the same time, his business, now boarded up, was also broken into, the floorboards pried up, and portions of the walls torn down. Clearly, someone was looking for his hoard of Lesher dollars.

Exactly where Zach Hutton cached his collection of Lesher dollars remains a mystery to this day, but it is presumed that they are buried somewhere on one of his former properties.

Today, the Lesher dollars are highly prized and considered to be very important by serious and professional coin collectors. In addition to the value of their silver content, they also possess considerable historical significance.

Depending on the type of coins, the Lesher dollars are valued today at between $650 and $6,000 apiece, with the $6,000 being applied to the 1901 coins bearing the business imprints and in mint condition. Since Lesher put away each new coin as he received it, it is presumed that most or all of them are still in mint condition. A coin collector who was consulted about the potential value of the lost Hutton collection estimated it would be worth at least $150,000 on the collectors' market today, and could be worth as much as a staggering $1,200,000!

LOST LAKE OF GOLD

Culebra Peak rises 14,069 feet above sea level near the western edge of Costilla County in southern Colorado. Culebra Peak is the tallest mountain in a string of peaks known locally as the Culebra Range. From time to time, prospectors have encountered gold in the Culebra Range but never enough to generate any significant mining operations. One day in April 1892, however, a man named Ashton B. Teeples camped near a lake located in a remote valley high up in the range that yielded unbelievable amounts of the precious metal. For the next three days, Teeples panned gold from the lake shore, ultimately filling all of his available packs with the rich ore. One very conservative estimate is that Teeples, in that very short time, accumulated a surprising two-and-a-half million dollars worth of gold at today's values!

After eventually running out of food, Teeples was forced to leave the mountain and return to civilization to rest, purchase supplies, and make plans to return to his lake of gold. In the process, he was attacked by highwaymen and nearly killed and was never able to make the return trip. To this day, the location of Ashton Teeples' lost lake of gold remains one of Colorado's greatest mysteries.

* * *

At forty-five years of age, Ashton Teeples had been a prospector and miner for twenty-seven years. During that time he recorded a number of successes and more than his share of failures as he pursued his quest to find a rich gold deposit. It was his search for gold that brought him to the Culebra Range in 1892.

One afternoon Teeples was leading his string of three burros down a remote valley in the Culebra range toward Whiskey Creek Pass when the region was struck by a severe and unexpected blizzard. The blinding snow, high winds, and stinging sleet made negotiating the trail very difficult. Years later, Teeples wrote in his journal that the snow and sleet were so thick for a time that he could not even see the burros walking next to him. Presently, during a brief period when the storm abated somewhat, Teeples spotted a recessed area near the base of an adjacent canyon wall. Leading the burros, he left the trail and stumbled toward this potential shelter. With great difficulty, he finally reached it, and was delighted to find that it did, in fact, afford some modicum of protection from the howling winds and falling snow.

Man and burros huddled together in the shallow shelter for most of the day. Finally, late in the afternoon the wind and snow died down and Teeples ventured out into the nearby forest to gather firewood. As he did so, the sky gradually cleared and the sun came out.

Teeples got a fire going about an hour before sundown. While he unloaded the packs from the burros and stashed his equipment near the rear of the rock alcove, he glanced out at the adjacent valley from time to time. His work done, he stood near the fire and relished the warmth of the blaze as he looked across the strange valley and contemplated the predicament in which he found himself. He had never been in this part of the range before. He estimated the walls of this huge, wide canyon reached upwards from the valley floor some 800 feet in height. The valley itself was round, almost bowl-shaped, and covered approximately 300 acres. In the center was a natural lake, about five to six acres in extent. Just as the sun was about to drop behind a ridge, the light that struck the lake reflected a golden color. Intrigued, Teeples decided he would walk down to the lake and examine it in the morning.

Following a breakfast of jerky the next morning, Teeples renewed his supply of firewood, saw that his burros had plenty of graze, picked up a gold pan, and walked over to the lake. Teeples was amazed at the clarity of the water; he could see the bottom of the lake over twenty yards from the shore. As was his habit when around water in these mountains, Teeples squatted down and panned up a couple handsful of small gravel at the waterline, swirled it around the pan, and dumped out the excess. After several swirls he was surprised to find a quantity of gold nuggets in the bottom of the pan. On examining them closely in the bright morning light, Teeples discovered they were quite pure and in surprising abundance. He placed the nuggets in a shirt pocket and panned for more.

Within forty-five minutes, Teeples had filled his shirt and pants pockets with gold nuggets, some of them as big as a pea. He returned to his campsite in the alcove, deposited all of the nuggets into a canvas ore sack, and returned to the lake for more.

For three days, working from dawn until dusk, Teeples panned approximately forty yards of the lake's shoreline. With each panning, he recovered a remarkable amount of gold, and at the end of that time, all of his sacks were full of nuggets and he was now placing them in coffee cans, tobacco pouches, and inside spare socks.

At the end of that three days, Teeples had run out of food. He spent a portion of one afternoon in search of some wild game but was unable to find any. Discouraged, he realized it would be necessary to return to civilization, sell his gold, and make preparations for a return trip to what he referred to as his golden lake.

After packing the burros, Teeples struck out for Whiskey Pass once again, finally reaching it after following a long and winding trail. From here, he continued along the path that led down through the foothills and onto the lowlands below, eventually arriving in the tiny settlement of Chama, New Mexico, a few miles to the west. He was very tired and hungry from not eating for two days. In Chama, he rested for nearly a week, keeping his gold filled packs in sight at all times. When he finally recovered enough to continue his journey, he loaded his burros, packed his gear, and traveled east to the town of Trinidad where he intended to convert his gold to cash.

Two hours out of Chama, Teeples, while walking at a leisurely pace and leading his three gold-laden burros, he spotted eight horsemen riding toward him on the trail. Just as he stepped to the side of the trail to allow the horsemen to pass, the newcomers pulled revolvers from their holsters and suddenly opened fire on the surprised Teeples. In defense, Teeples pulled his own weapon and returned the fire, killing one of the attackers with the first shot and causing the rest to seek cover behind some nearby rocks. As the riders dismounted and reloaded their weapons, Teeples pulled a rifle from a scabbard that hung from one of the burros. As the attackers stepped out from behind the rocks and warily approached Teeples on foot, the miner leveled his rifle and killed another one, wounded yet another, and caused their fellows to scurry away once again. Quickly, Teeples led his burros behind some boulders a short distance from the trail.

For the next hour, Teeples exchanged gunfire with the riders. One by one, the attackers crept forward under cover until three of them were within twenty-five feet of their intended victim. When one carrying a rifle rose up to try for a clear shot at Teeples, the miner reacted quickly and shot his attacker in the head, killing him instantly. With half of their force now dead, the remaining highwaymen returned to their horses, mounted up, and rode away.

Teeples remained hiding behind the boulders until nightfall, worried that his attackers might be waiting for him somewhere down the road. Finally, reasonably convinced they were gone, Teeples pulled his burros back onto the road. He had not proceeded far when, suspicious an ambush lay somewhere ahead, Teeples left the trail and followed a far more difficult, but safer, route toward Trinidad. He traveled all night without sleep. By sunrise he was exhausted but still cautious. He found a rock overhang, tied his burros inside, crawled into one corner, and fell asleep. For the next three days, in an effort to elude anyone who might be looking for him and his gold, Teeples traveled by night and hid during the day.

On the morning of his fourth day of travel, Teeples was only a few miles to the west of the town of Boncarbo when shots rang out. The miner, struck twice in the thigh and once in the left shoulder, toppled to the ground. Dazed and in pain, he managed to drag himself into the shelter of some nearby rocks.

When he rose from his hiding place, Teeples watched in horror as his burros, frightened by the sudden gunfire, raced back up the trail. At the same time, his attackers, mounted and with guns blazing, were riding hard toward his position. Weakly, Teeples raised his revolver and fired at the oncoming bandits. His first shot struck one and knocked him from the saddle. As Teeples continued firing, he was struck thrice more, and dropped to the ground, unconscious.

Some time later, Teeples awoke, painfully aware of a deep and throbbing headache. While he was trying to focus his eyes, he heard voices speaking in Spanish. Fearing he was being held prisoner by Mexican bandidos, he remained quiet and still until he was eventually approached.

A young Mexican approached and handed him a cup of coffee. In halting English, the Mexican explained that he and a companion, both sheepherders, had found him on the trail bleeding badly. They also found two dead bandits along with two dead horses. The sheepherders had cleaned Teeples' wounds and dressed them with an herb concoction that inhibited infection somewhat.

When Teeples finally recovered enough to sit up, he looked around and asked about his burros. One of the Mexicans told him they found his three burros a short distance up the trail. They were returned to this camp, he explained, their packs removed, and the animals led out to a nearby pasture to graze. The sheepherder told Teeples that it was very dangerous to travel with so much gold when there were so many robbers on the roads. He assured Teeples that none of the gold was taken and that they would help him pack it up when he was ready to leave.

Two days later, though still stiff and hurting from his wounds, Teeples was escorted by the sheepherders to a small village about two miles away. Here he was turned over to an aged Mexican who cleaned and redressed his wounds and insisted the prospector rest for a few more days. Two days later, it began to look as though one of Teeples' legs was badly infected and might have to be amputated. Placing him in a wagon, along with his packs of gold, the old Mexican transported him to a small railroad station. When the train stopped for water and fuel, Teeples and his packs were placed aboard and transported to Trinidad where he was admitted to the small hospital there.

While recovering in the hospital, Teeples arranged for the sale of his gold, and a few days later he received a check for $225,000.

Teeples told his doctor and the Trinidad sheriff the circumstances that led to his arrival in Trinidad. Intrigued at the prospect of so much gold lying in a lake somewhere in the Culebra Range, the two men asked for directions. Teeples agreed to tell them what he knew, stating he never wanted to return to the valley. As well as he could remember, Teeples informed them of his route when leaving the range, and admitted that he was lost when he encountered the golden lake.

Together, the sheriff and the doctor arranged an expedition into the Culebras to try to find the lake of gold, and though they remained in the area for six weeks they were unable to locate it. The sheriff, Tomas Santos, made three more attempts during the next four years to find the lake but with no success.

With his money from the sale of the gold, Teeples purchased a large farm near his hometown in Kansas. Five years later, Teeples was visited by Santos, now the former sheriff from Trinidad. Santos explained that he had fallen on hard times and wished to make at least one more attempt at locating the golden lake. Teeples sympathized with the man who had treated him well while he was in the hospital, and agreed to help him find it. Several days later, Teeples, Santos, and Teeples' step-son Harold returned to Colorado and the Culebra Range.

When the three men arrived at Trinidad they heard a most amazing story. Some two years earlier, an old man, a long-time prospector in the area, was found in a crude camp somewhere between the mountain range and the settlement of Segundo, located about twenty-five miles east of Culebra Peak. When a party of hunters approached his camp, they found the old man severely dehydrated and apparently dying. Nearby was a leather pack filled with gold. Before he died, the old man told the hunters the gold came from a lake high up in the Culebra Mountains. He said there was more gold in the lake than he could pan in a lifetime.

For six weeks, Teeples, Santos, and the step-son traveled and searched the Culebra Mountains for the golden lake. They found a number of lakes high in the range, all filled with clear water from melting snows, but none were the lake of Teeples' experience.

The three men eventually arrived in a roughly circular, high canyon that Teeples was certain was the correct location. Excitedly he led his two companions to where he believed the lake to be but found only rock and rubble. Years later, Teeples wrote that he was convinced an earthquake in the area had generated rockslides from the adjacent mountainsides, rockslides which covered up the golden lake.

If Teeples was correct, the lake still lies somwehere in the higher reaches of the Culebra Mountains, buried beneath tons of rock and debris.

If the former lake is as rich with gold as Teeples claimed, it may well be worth the effort to remove the accumulation of rock that has covered it, for the evidence strongly suggests that wealth beyond imagination lies just below.

ROADSIDE GOLD MINE

Not far from the south-central Colorado town of Salida lies a lost gold mine, one that has a proven vein of gold of great value. Far from being remote and difficult to reach like many lost mines, this one is located a comparatively short distance from the busy Highway 50. It was discovered accidentally in 1938 by three men who were completely unaware of its potential. Several years passed before they learned the rock they dug from the mine was, in fact, a very high quality gold. When they decided to return to the mine, they were unable to find it.

* * *

It was early autumn in 1938 as a road crew worked on a section of Colorado State Highway 50 a few miles southeast of Salida near the border of Chaffee and Fremont counties. As the eight men stopped for their lunch break, they were informed by the supervisor that some important equipment they were waiting for had been delayed another three to four hours. Since work could not proceed without the necessary machinery, the supervisor gave the men most of the afternoon off.

Three of the workers—Ed Ebersol, Paul Lalire, and

Richard Tyler—decided to hike into a nearby canyon to search for signs of game. Each season, the three men went deer hunting together and were constantly on the lookout for new locations.

Deer sign was abundant as the three men made their way up the low, narrow canyon. Clear water flowed down a small stream that wound along the floor of the canyon, and trees provided cover. As they hiked, the men noticed they were on some kind of a trail. It was much too wide for a game trail—it seemed wide enough to accommodate a wagon—and it appeared as though it hadn't been used in years. Curious, the three friends decided to follow it on up the canyon.

As the trio followed the winding trail up the steepening slope near the upper end of the canyon, they spotted an entrance to a mine along with an associated talus pile at a point where it appeared the trail came to an end. They hurried on and soon found themselves standing in front of the mine, the air at the opening noticeably cooler than that outside. They leaned into the shaft and tried to peer into the darkness beyond, but could see nothing. Lalire fashioned a crude torch from some nearby pine branches and grasses, lit it, and the three men passed into the tunnel.

It soon became obvious that this mine had been abandoned for a long time, for thick layers of dust covered the floor and various outcrops encountered along the way. Thick timbers shoring the excavation were passed, timbers apparently cut and shaped by hand for adze marks were clearly visible along their sides. About fifteen yards into the shaft, Tyler's boot struck an object on the floor. Picking it up, he discovered it was a very old and rusted miner's pick. A search of the floor of the tunnel at the their feet yielded several more tools—two hammers, another pick, a well worn shovel with a broken handle, and three long, wide rock chisels. According to Lalire many years later, the tools appeared as if they had been dropped in place as miners suddenly stopped working and left the mine. Furthermore, the tools appeared to be very old, of a kind and quality not seen in a century or more, causing the men to suspect the mine may have been worked generations earlier by Spaniards.

When their torch was almost burned out, Ebersol, Lalire, and Tyler left the cave and explored the slope outside. Near the base of the slope and a few yards off the trail they found a rectangle of rocks that had apparently once been part of the foundation of a former habitation. Among the debris, they found several old rotted juniper logs that had been notched and likely part of the original structure. Perhaps, the three men considered, they were looking upon the remains of a very old log cabin, long since tumbled down and a victim of the elements.

A few steps from the rock rectangle was a circular firepit. The three friends deduced that whoever worked the mine lived down here. The location seemed ideal— fresh water in the stream, plenty of game, and the narrow canyon itself offered shelter from storms.

Tyler considered that life here must have been good for the miners and wondered aloud why they left. Ebersol said one reason miners leave a site is because they have exhausted the supply of whatever it was they were mining. Tyler responded that even if they left for that reason, they would have taken their tools with them and not just dropped them on the floor of the tunnel. Such a thing, continued Tyler, suggested a hurried, maybe even a panicked, departure.

Perhaps they were attacked by Indians, offered Ebersol. It was well known among those who studied such things that the Indians who lived in this area were very hostile to the intrusion of white settlers, traders, trappers, and particularly miners.

The three men explored around the floor of the canyon in the area of the old campsite looking for evidence of what may have occurred here, but found nothing substantive. Tyler then suggested they return to the shaft, follow it to its end, and see if they could discern what it was that was mined.

After making more torches, the three men re-entered the shaft and cautiously followed it along its length. After passing the scattered pile of tools they encountered earlier, they encountered something that caused them to recoil in sudden shock and horror—a human skeleton. Most of the bones appeared to have been chewed away by rodents, but the skull was, for the most part, intact.

At the rear of the mine, they found a three-inch thick vein of quartz with some kind of mineral running through it. They could not tell what it was, but they dug out several pieces and placed them in their pockets. They agreed they would take the samples to someone knowledgeable and have them identified.

Since they had been in the canyon for approximately four hours, the three companions decided it was time to return to work. By the time they had hiked back to the road, the equipment they were waiting on had arrived and work proceeded for another two hours.

While riding in a car on the way home after work that evening, the rock samples were all handed over to Ebersol who claimed he knew someone who could identify them.

For the next two months, the road crew worked on highway maintenance, gradually moving toward the southeast and getting farther and farther away from the canyon where Ebersol, Lalire, and Tyler found the old mine shaft.

Ebersol placed the rock samples in a metal bucket in the basement of his house with the intention of having them examined in the near future. During the next few weeks, however, the three friends began making preparations for the coming hunting season, became involved with a variety of events at their children's schools, and remained busy with their jobs at the highway department. As time passed, they eventually forgot about the rock samples.

Three years later, the three men moved to Alamosa, located approximately eighty miles south of Salida. Ebersol and Lalire continued to work for the state highway department and Lalire took a job with the railroad. Approximately six years after finding the old mine, Ebersol encountered the bucket of rocks in his basement and finally decided to have them examined. He took them to a friend who worked as a state geologist. After intently studying each piece of quartz, the friend informed Ebersol that they contained quite a bit of gold. He recommended Ebersol have the rock assayed by a professional, and gave him the address of a man with whom he regularly conducted business. Ebersol delivered the rocks to the assayer. Three weeks later the assayer called him and informed him the quartz was laced with a high grade of gold. The assayer told Ebersol that the gold was quite pure, that it was easily separated from the quartz matrix, and that if there was more where he found this then he would be a very rich man indeed.

Excited by this news, Ebersol immediately contacted Lalire and Tyler, informing them of their good fortune. That weekend, the three men met and made plans to return to the canyon where they found the mine and begin extracting the gold.

Before the weekend arrived, however, Tyler was killed in an automobile accident. Several more weeks passed before Ebersol and Lalire felt they were ready to travel to the mine.

Early one Saturday morning they left Alamosa, drove north to Salida, then followed Highway 50 southeast out of town. Since they had last traveled this road it had been changed somewhat—curves had been straightened and inclines leveled. As they drove through the vaguely familiar landscape, they had difficulty identifying the exact canyon in which they hiked that afternoon six years earlier.

Finally they decided on one particular canyon that appeared to satisfy their recollections, but when they approached the entrance to it was fenced off. Hanging from the top wire of the fence was a sign that read "PRIVATE PROPERTY, KEEP OFF." Beneath the sign was another on which was printed the name of a ranch.

At first, the two friends were inclined to climb the fence and hike to the rear of the canyon to determine if, in fact, it was the correct one. After debating it for a moment, they decided instead to contact the owner of the ranch and attempted to obtain permission to do so.

They had no success finding the rancher that day and returned home to Alamosa, disappointed and dejected. It was, in fact, three weeks before they were able to place a call to the rancher. Not wanting to alert the rancher to the prospect that there might be a very rich gold mine on his property, they initially said they called to request permission to hunt. The rancher refused, explaining that some of his livestock were in that canyon and he didn't want to chance an accidental bullet finding one of them.

With no alternative, the two then asked the rancher for permission to enter the canyon in order to examine and possibly dig some minerals from the old mine that existed there. The rancher replied that he was unaware of any mine in the canyon and hung up.

For the rest of their lives, Ebersol and Lalire remained convinced that the mine was in that very canyon and that it contained an abundance of gold that could make them rich men. Being law-abiding citizens, however, they could not bring themselves to trespass onto the rancher's property.

Ebersol and Lalire went to their graves wondering what life might have been like if they had been granted permission to dig gold from the old abandoned mine, gold that apparently still lies within the quartz matrix found at the rear of the mysterious tunnel.

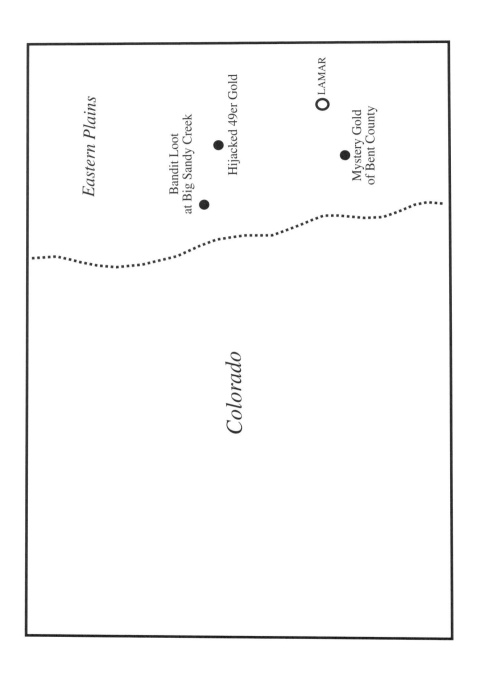

Eastern Plains

Bandit Loot
at Big Sandy Creek

Hijacked 49er Gold

LAMAR

Mystery Gold
of Bent County

Colorado

THE EASTERN PLAINS

Geographically, the eastern plains of Colorado are as different from the Rocky Mountains and the Western Slope as night is from day. Instead of rugged peaks, steep slopes, high mountain passes, and outcrops of an immeasurable variety of ore, the eastern plains extend from the eastern side of the Rocky Mountains to the Kansas and Nebraska borders and beyond. In the geographic context, the word "plain" means flat, and indeed, when compared to the nearly vertical prominences of the grand Rockies to the west, the eastern plains are, indeed, fairly horizonal, relatively level, and, in places, even quite smooth.

Many confuse the term flat with featureless, and the eastern plains of Colorado are anything but. Composed in large part of sediment eroded from the Rockies and washed eastward via the dominant drainage patterns, these plains are essentially treeless save for the river courses. It is these many rivers and streams, however, that provide a great deal of the character to the eastern plains.

The most prominent of these rivers, of course, is the Arkansas. Born of melting snow and glacier on a mountain near Leadville, the icy cold waters rush down the eastern slopes of the Rockies until reaching the plains. Here, with a much gentler gradient, the river slows and passes through cities and towns such as Pueblo, La Junta, Las Animas, and Lamar before entering Kansas on its way to its confluence with the mighty Mississippi several hundred miles to the east.

Other significant rivers and streams include the Republican River and its many forks, the Purgatorie River, the South Platte River, Rush Creek, the beginnings of the Smoky Hill River, and others. Most of these streams flow essentially eastward, following the gently sloping gradient. Before the coming of the white settlers, they flowed through prairies thick and deep with native grasses, but now bisect plowed fields and pastures. These rivers and streams have cut into the prairie substrate, often creating deep canyons, and providing surprising variety to the plains.

While there is no mining of ore to speak of in the eastern plains of Colorado, a great deal of gold and silver was transported across its surface. Carried by travelers, miners, and outlaws, much of it never arrived at the intended destination and was sometimes lost, buried, and many times forgotten.

Fortunes were deposited on the Colorado plains in this manner, many of which remain today where they were placed or abandoned decades earlier.

Part of America's Great Plains, the eastern plains of Colorado are a semi-arid grassland, a type of landscape most often associated with Kansas and Nebraska.

Semi-arid they may be, but they are also a rich and fertile setting for colorful and compelling tales of lost and buried treasures, many of which continue to entice people into these environs in search of their fortunes and in pursuit of their dreams.

BANDIT LOOT BURIED AT BIG SANDY CREEK

On August 6, 1900, a Union Pacific train carrying passengers and freight was robbed as it chugged along not far from Hugo, Colorado. During the robbery, one man was killed, and the robbers fled with a gunny sack filled with watches, rings, and money taken from the passengers. In addition, twelve gold bars valued, according to a newspaper report, at $35,000 were also carried away.

Though the robbers were captured and subsequently killed during an escape attempt, the location of the hidden booty remains a mystery.

* * *

When the Union Pacific train stopped at Lake Station, some fifteen miles west of Hugo in Lincoln County, two men were waiting in the shadows of the water tank. Lake Station consisted only of the tank, a coal chute, and a small shed. Here, the train took on coal and water on its eastward journey toward Kansas. As one of the railroad workers capped off the water tank and returned the hose to the metal hook from which it hung, the two men waiting behind the tank stepped out and quietly boarded the train.

Before entering one of the passenger coaches, the two newcomers placed masks over their faces, drew revolvers, and approached conductor D. D. Smith. At gunpoint, Smith was marched toward the baggage car where he was ordered to point out the location of twelve large gold ingots. After doing so, one of the masked men stuffed the gold bars into gunny sacks, while the other opened a side door. The bars were then stacked near the opening.

Leaving conductor Smith in the baggage car, the two gunmen then entered the nearest passenger car, the Lebo, and casually informed the travelers that they were being held up. As one of the outlaws pointed his revolver at the passengers, the other moved slowly among the stunned victims as they dropped watches, rings, wallets, pistols, and other valuables into a sack. From this car, the gunmen moved to the next and repeated the procedure.

In the third car, one of the robbers pulled aside the curtain to a sleeping berth and was immediately confronted by passenger William Fay. Fay, a former official with the Denver Gas Company, raised up, and was reaching for his pistol when the robber shot him square in the mouth, killing him instantly. The robbers fired four more shots in quick succession in an attempt to frighten the remaining passengers, then proceeded to rob them.

Several minutes later, the train slowed down as it approached the railroad depot at Hugo. As it did, the gunmen, carrying heavy sacks of valuables, moved back toward the baggage car. Just as the train pulled to a stop, the robbers tossed the gold bars and the sacks of valuables onto the ground, jumped from the train, and ran into a nearby copse of trees. Seconds later they reappeared, each riding a horse and leading another. Hurriedly, they loaded the gunny sacks onto the horses and rode away.

At the first opportunity, conductor Smith telegraphed

railroad officials who made a quick assessment of the situation. After determining one murder was committed along with the theft of the valuable gold shipment and passengers' valuables, Hugo Sheriff John Freeman was quickly summoned. Freeman, along with six newly deputized men, was requested by the railroad to ride out in pursuit of the outlaws and retrieve the gold. By the time Freeman and his posse got under way, however, the bandits had a two-hour head start.

Farther down the railroad line, the sheriff of Cheyenne Wells in Cheyenne County, J. R. Groff, received a telegram informing him of the robbery and murder and alerting him to the prospect that the bandits might be headed his way. The Pinkerton Detective Agency in Denver was also notified. In a short time, a description of the two robbers was distributed throughout the area along with a notice announcing a $1,000 reward for their capture.

One of the outlaws was described as being five feet eight inches tall, slender, wearing dark clothes and an old hat. The other was identified as being short, baby-faced, thin, approximately forty years old, and wearing a black suit. It was also believed that the robbers were Indians, or at least part Indian.

By noon of the following day, every railroad town in eastern Colorado and western Kansas had been alerted to be on the lookout for the bandits. The eastern Colorado countryside was being searched by several posses of lawmen.

On August 8, two men believed to be the train robbers were arrested some thirty-five miles away northwest of Hugo in Ebert County. The two—Mart Sides and Fred Merrick—matched the published descriptions of the bandits. Neither was able to provide an acceptable alibi and both had substantial criminal records. Sides and Merrick were arrested and charged with robbery and murder. When taken into custody, neither was in possession of the gold bars or the valuables taken from the Union Pacific train.

At first, Sides and Merrick vehemently denied having anything to do with robbing the train, but finally relented and admitted their involvement. When pressed for information relative to what had become of the gold and the passengers' valuables, they claimed they buried them in a sandbank next to the Big Sandy Creek shortly after entering Ebert County. Despite exhaustive questioning by lawmen, the two men refused to provide any specific directions to the hidden loot.

Two days later while Sides and Merrick were being transported to Goodland, Kansas, to await trial, they snatched revolvers from two of their guards and attempted to escape. During the ensuing gunfight between the prisoners and the guards, Sides was killed. Merrick evaded the guards, stole a horse, and rode away, finally taking refuge in a ranch house a short time later.

When lawmen, following Merrick's trail, arrived at the ranch house they were fired on by the outlaw. After several minutes of unsuccessfully trying to coax Merrick into giving up, the lawmen decided to set fire to the house. Accounts of subsequent events are unclear as to whether Merrick was killed as he attempted to flee from the burning house or if he perished within. In any event, he was pronounced dead at the scene.

With the deaths of Merrick and Sides went any knowledge of where the gold bars and the sacks of valuables were buried. All that is known is that the location was somewhere west of the town of Limon near Big Sandy Creek in Ebert County. The banks of the Big Sandy were searched by lawmen for days but nothing was ever found.

Today, modern prospectors armed with metal detectors have ranged along the banks of the creek in search of the gold, but haven't located any of it.

It may be that the normal meandering processes of the creek have obscured the hiding place of the loot. Others have suggested that the heavy weight of the gold and valuables may have actually caused the cache to sink deep into the soft and unconsolidated sands of the flood plain to a depth where metal detectors cannot reach.

Still others who maintain a more optimistic viewpoint suggest that someday the meandering action of the Big Sandy Creek may eventually uncover the buried loot, leaving it exposed to some lucky hiker or treasure hunter who happens to wander by the old cache at the right time.

HIJACKED 49ER GOLD
BURIED ON COLORADO PLAINS

Following the discovery of gold at Sutter's Mill in northern California in 1848, tens of thousands of hopeful miners, each seeking to get rich in a short amount of time by digging and panning for the ore, migrated to the Golden State from America's East and South. Along with the hopeful miners came businessmen, entrepreneurs, ministers, blacksmiths, prostitutes, politicians, and, of course, outlaws.

Gold was found, tons of it, but relatively few of those who made the long trek from the east were successful. Most of them failed in their attempts to find and mine gold in sufficient quantities, and a large percentage of them returned home broken and dispirited.

Mining gold was not the only way to get rich. A great deal of the ore that was excavated from the rocks and panned from the streams was simply stolen from the hardworking miners by outlaws. This tale concerns a gang of such outlaws who made a fortune stealing gold from hapless miners and, on making their way back east, were forced to bury it as a result of pursuit from lawmen. One of the outlaws eventually returned for this sizeable hoard many years later, but was never able to find it. The gold still lies just beneath the surface of the prairie where it was placed well over a century ago.

* * *

The year was 1857, and the gang of eight men found themselves wealthy beyond their wildest imaginations. For the previous three years they had raided small mining camps along the placer streams in northern California, taking gold at gunpoint from the men who worked so hard to retrieve it. Those who refused to turn over their gold were simply killed on the spot, and it has been estimated that at least two dozen placer miners met their fate in this manner at the hands of these outlaws.

As the numbers of lawmen in the area increased, and as more and more of the placer miners began arming themselves against such attacks, the bandits decided it was time to quit and return to their homes in the east and live out the remainder of their lives as wealthy men. After purchasing supplies for the long journey, they set out, trailed by several packhorses that transported their ill-gotten gains.

Uneventful weeks passed as the eight men made their way through the Rocky Mountains and began the long trek across the Great Plains. Arriving at the eastern Colorado settlement of Hugo, they decided to rest themselves and their horses for a few days before continuing.

While they repaired gear, renewed supplies, and availed themselves of the whiskey and women Hugo had to offer, the bandits learned of a soon-to-arrive stagecoach carrying a large military payroll. Convinced it would be an easy task to stop the stage and hijack the payroll, the eight began to make plans to add to their already impressive wealth.

Two days later, with their gold-carrying pack horses in

tow, they rode from behind a copse of trees along the trail leading to Hugo and forced the incoming stagecoach to a stop. The outlaws, however, were surprised by, and quite unprepared for, the military escort that accompanied the stage. The troopers, six in all, but much better armed than the outlaws, had the immediate advantage and opened fire on the attackers, killing two outright, seriously wounding another, and sending the rest riding away as fast as they could make their horses and mules go.

After grabbing the lead ropes to the pack horses, the five outlaws who survived the initial fusillade from the troopers fled south as fast as possible. While three of the troopers continued with the stage on to Hugo, the three others set off in pursuit of the outlaws. During the chase, three more outlaws were killed.

Even though the outlaws were leading the cumbersome and heavily laden packhorses, all of their stock was well-rested from the respite of several days in Hugo. The pursuing soldiers, on the other hand, were riding horses weary from the long trip with the stagecoach, and it wasn't long before they fell behind.

Nearing the Smoky Hill Trail not far from the small community of Clifford, the two surviving bandits found themselves well ahead of the pursuit and decided to stop and rest. Realizing the gold-laden packhorses were slowing them down, they decided to bury the loot and return for it another time. Quickly, they excavated a wide, deep hole into which they placed the gold. Following this, they then created three phony graves arranged in a triangle with the gold in the center. At the head of each grave they placed a crudely fashioned stone slab. The surviving bandits chiseled their names onto two of the slabs and on the third scratched the word "Unknown." On each they scratched the year: 1857. This done, they turned the pack-horses loose, mounted up, and rode away.

As far as is known, the two men got away, presumably to their homes in the east.

In the year 1884, a stranger arrived at Clifford. Since few visitors ever came to this tiny settlement, the event was easily remembered by several residents many years later. For the most part, the stranger spoke little and generally kept to himself, but on occasion he would ask someone if they knew of a place nearby where there were three graves arranged in a triangle. No one knew of such a place, and the citizens of Clifford considered this a rather unusual question. When not in his small campsite just on the edge of the settlement, the stranger was often seen riding across the landscape as if searching for something.

Presently, he moved his camp to Hugo and began asking the same questions. A short time later, Hugo residents spotted him riding around the grassy prairie as if he were looking for something in particular. After several days in Hugo, the stranger became friends with resident James Will. From time to time, the stranger would invite Will to accompany him on his rides across the plains in search of the three graves. Will did so, and as the two men grew closer, the stranger identified himself as Joseph Lowe and eventually admitted he was one of the bandits who buried the gold at the center of the three graves.

For several more weeks the two men searched for the graves but never found them. Presently, Lowe rode away, never to return.

In 1931, a Hugo resident named Elkins reported he found an old stone slab headstone out on the prairie, hidden among the weeds and tall grass. The stone was quite weathered, but one could just barely make out the date

1857 scratched onto the front. Those in Hugo old enough to remember the visit of the stranger almost fifty years earlier recounted the tale of the buried gold. Before long, a number of people were searching the area for the buried loot.

In 1934, someone found a second headstone near the place where the first was discovered. This one bore the name "Joseph Foxe Lowe," and the date "Aug. 8, 1857." The finder was not aware of the story of the buried gold and simply left the stone where he found it. Several years later when he learned the truth behind the graves and the gold associated with it, he tried to relocate the headstone but was unable to find it.

In 1984, this same headstone was found once again, but as before the finder had no inkling of the tale of buried gold that was associated with it. The only directional information provided was that the stone was discovered out on the prairie not far from the old settlement of Clifford.

In spite of the occasional discovery of the location of the bizarre little graveyard, the buried gold has never been recovered. What may amount to well over one million dollars worth of the precious metal still lies just a few inches below the surface of the eastern Colorado prairie.

MYSTERY GOLD OF BENT COUNTY

One of the strangest tales of lost gold in Colorado, one that remains an unsolved mystery to this day, is set in Bent County. While the actual location has been debated over the many decades that have passed, most agree that it took place along the Purgatorie River several miles upstream from its confluence with the Arkansas River.

The time was the early 1830s, and, save for some nomadic Indians, the only people living in this area were those associated with Bent's Fort, located approximately ten miles west of present-day Las Animas.

Years earlier, this region was visited by trappers intent on supplying beaver and other pelts to the burgeoning market in the East and in Europe. In 1832, two brothers, Charles and William Bent, built a trading post next to the Arkansas River. Here, they supplied needed goods to the trappers and, in turn, purchased their furs which were shipped eastward by wagon. As trade increased in the area, the fort became a common stopover for haulers transporting freight to Santa Fe. Years later, it served numerous wagon trains heading west.

It was during the first years the fort was in business that trappers occasionally spotted a black wagon pulled by six black horses moving at a high rate of speed along the road that paralleled the Purgatorie River about ten miles southeast of the fort. From the distance that they observed the wagon, the trappers noted that the driver appeared to be dressed in black and was whipping the horses to greater and greater speeds. Several times the wagon was spotted, always at night, and when the trappers attempted to hail the driver, he responded only by increasing his speed, apparently intent on placing as much distance from himself and the Frenchmen as possible.

Late one evening, one of the trappers was riding down the road when he spotted the oncoming wagon. Pulling to the side, he waved at the driver as he sped by, never looking up and never acknowledging the presence of the man on horseback. The trapper later stated that the driver appeared to be a Spaniard, though how he could ascertain such a thing in the dark of night is anyone's guess.

On another occasion when a pair of trappers pulled to the side of the road to allow the speeding wagon to pass, something occurred to deepen the mystery of the strange wagon and its driver. As the trappers watched the wagon race off into the distance along the bumpy road that followed the river, they noted several objects fall out of the back. Curious, they rode to where the objects lay in the road, dismounted and examined them, and were stunned to discover they were gold ingots—six of them!

The next morning the trappers carried the ingots to Bent's Fort and told everyone present what had occurred. Intrigued and excited, Bent's Fort customers were determined to remain on the lookout for the mysterious black wagon. Unfortunately for them, many weeks passed before it was seen again.

The next time the wagon was spotted, the trappers were well over a mile away. By the time they reached the trail and took up pursuit, the wagon, with such a great head start, was long gone. Rather than chase the wagon and its mysterious driver, they decided to backtrack to try to discover where it came from.

For several miles the wagon tracks were followed until at last the trappers came to a place where it appeared the vehicle entered the main road from a little used trail that led back into a rather rugged-looking canyon. For the next several hours, the trappers explored up and down the canyon but found nothing. Here and there along the canyon walls were several shallow caves; a few were examined but little was discovered save for packrat nests.

The black wagon and driver were seen several times more during the ensuing years but, as before, no one ever got close enough to get a good look at the driver or the load that was being transported.

Sometime during the early 1850s, a stranger arrived in the area of Bent's Fort and remained for several days camped outside its walls. Two years earlier he traveled to California from someplace in the East. Like many hopeful young men of the time, he had dreams of striking gold in the California fields and returning home a wealthy man. And, like many other young men, it was not to be and so he undertook the long journey home.

So broke was he that he traveled on foot, and it took him many months to reach the eastern plains of Colorado where he was determined to rest for several days before reembarking on his journey.

While camped near Bent's Fort, the young man heard the tales of the mysterious black wagon that was apparently transporting gold ingots from one location to another. He entertained himself by hiking along the Purgatorie River near where it confluences with the Arkansas River, all the while thinking he might find some clue as to the origin of the gold.

Entering the canyon of the lower Purgatorie, the young man encountered several caves and decided to investigate them. Most of the caves were empty but one yielded an interesting discovery. As the young man entered the deep, wide cave—actually a recessed area in the rock under an overhang—he encountered the remains of an old fire pit, one that had not been used for approximately twenty years, he estimated. Kicking around in the dirt near the fire pit, he found what appeared to be several clay tiles, clearly of Spanish origin. He placed them in his coat pocket.

At the rear of the cave and partially buried under blowsand he found an old wooden chest with iron fittings. Inside, he discovered a handful of gold coins, again of Spanish origin. Near the chest he also found the remains of a rotten leather harness fitted with silver conchos.

It was growing late in the day, and the young man realized he must set out immediately in order to reach his camp by nightfall. After scooping out a shallow hole in the floor of the cave, he buried the chest, coins, tiles, and harness. He kicked apart the circle of stones that ringed the firepit and scattered the ashes, mixing them with the sand in the cave. Convinced he was at or near the location from which the mysterious man in black loaded gold ingots into his wagon, he was intent on removing the evidence lest another might stumble upon the same clues. Into a nearby tree, the young man marked the cave by thrusting two belt knives into the trunk, each pointing toward the opening.

As he made his way back down the trail that led to the main road, the young man spied yet another cave, a much smaller and less obvious one, he had not seen before.

Curious to see if it might hold more clues, or even the gold itself, he started for it.

Clambering up the steeply angled talus slope at the mouth of the cave, he fell and shattered his left leg. In great pain, he managed to drag himself up the rocky slope and into the mouth of the cave. There, along the back wall, he saw dozens of gold ingots stacked like cordwood. Moments later, he passed out and remained unconscious for approximately twenty-four hours.

When at last he awoke, the young man proceeded to drag himself out of the cave, down the slope, and along the trail to the main road. Several hours later, he was found by a pair of travelers who placed him in a wagon and transported him to a small Mexican settlement on the banks of the Arkansas River. Here his leg was set and his now raging fever was treated with herb concoctions.

During one of his lucid periods, the young man told of his discovery—the chest, the coins, the harness, the tiles, and the stacks of gold ingots. He spoke of how he marked the location with his belt knives and how he intended to return to the site, retrieve the gold, and return home a rich man.

Unfortunately, the young man did not recover and died in his sleep the following night, and with his death went the secret to the location of the cave that contained the gold ingots.

The Mystery Gold of Bent County, as it has come to be called, has been the object of hundreds of searches during the past century-and-a-half. This cache of gold is aptly named, for it's location continues to elude searchers to this day.

THE AUTHOR

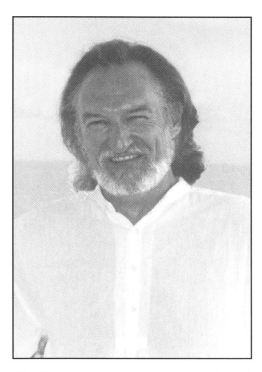

W. C. Jameson is a professional treasure hunter and an award-winning author of more than thirty-five books.

Other Books about Colorado
From CAXTON PRESS

Jeep Trails to Colorado Ghost Towns
ISBN 0-87004-021-9
8 1/4x5 1/2, 105 photographs, endsheet map,
245 pages, paper, $12.95

Ghost Towns of the Colorado Rockies
ISBN 0-87004-342-0

6x9, 401 pages, 136 photos, paper $17.95

Pioneers of the Colorado Parks
ISBN 0-87004-381-1

6x9, 276 pages, 45 illustrations, 4 maps, paper $17.95

From the Grave: A Roadside Guide
to Colorado's Pioneer Cemeteries
ISBN 0-87004-386-2 (paper) $24.95
ISBN 0-87004-390-0 (cloth) $34.95

6x9, 500 pages, 100 illustrations, maps

Our Ladies of the Tenderloin
Colorado's Legends in Lace
ISBN 0-87004-444-3

6x9, 200 pages, photographs, Paper $16.95

Colorado Ghost Towns
Past and Present
ISBN 0-87004-218-1

6x9, 322 pages, 140 illustrations, map, paper $14.95

For a free Caxton catalog write to:

CAXTON PRESS
312 Main Street
Caldwell, ID 83605-3299

or

Visit our Internet Website:

www.caxtonpress.com

Caxton Press is a division of The CAXTON PRINTERS, Ltd.